44 Questions for Black America

44 Questions for Black America

Written by Byron F. Wilson

iUniverse, Inc.
New York Lincoln Shanghai

44 Questions for Black America

Copyright © 2005 by Byron F. Wilson

iUniverse books may be ordered through booksellers or by contacting:

iUniverse
2021 Pine Lake Road, Suite 100
Lincoln, NE 68512
www.iuniverse.com
1-800-Authors (1-800-288-4677)

ISBN-13: 978-0-595-35592-1 (pbk)
ISBN-13: 978-0-595-80076-6 (ebk)
ISBN-10: 0-595-35592-7 (pbk)
ISBN-10: 0-595-80076-9 (ebk)

Printed in the United States of America

Acknowledgements

Family:

To my wife and everything, Tiffany: You are more than I ever imagined I could find in a partner. I sometimes wish that when people look at you they could see all the things that make you so great. All they can see is your alluring eyes and beautiful smile, although your beauty is quite impressive. But they don't know what a beautiful mind you have. A part of me thinks you might actually be smarter than I am. You hold me down (for those of you who don't know slang, that's a good thing.) and help me to make better decisions. You help me to deal with the everyday stresses of my life. You taught me that if I would focus on my own life first, that everything would fall into place. You have done nothing but support me in all my endeavors, which isn't always easy to do. You believe in both my writing and my mission. I can put no price on that. But most importantly, you have taught me how to live life. You make me happy. Thank you.

To my daughter Khelsei: I know your mom doesn't want to hear it, but I think you're turning out to be a Daddy's Girl. I love you more than I'll ever be able to explain, and I would readily give my life for yours. Never let anyone tell you that because you don't live with me, that you have anything less than anyone else. I will always be your father, and I'll always do the best with the time I have with you. Hopefully you will someday be as proud of me as I am of you. I don't have to tell you how special you are, but in time, you'll prove it to the world.

To Tyler and Kennedy: You both have taught me what it means to be a father. I know you didn't have to accept me; but you did. Some people marry a woman with children and then make the separation between their kids and her kids. But as for me, the only thing that's different is your blood. In my eyes and heart, I have four daughters. That will never change. Once you two grow up, you'll understand that being a stepparent isn't the easiest thing in the world to do. But you lovely ladies have made it pretty simple. I love you both.

To my unborn daughter: As of right now, your name is supposed to be Sydney. But who knows what it'll be by the time you are born. You're the first daughter I have that I'll get to raise from the beginning in the same household with your mother. I know that sounds *ghetto*, but it is what it is. I cannot express how excited I am about being your father. Anyway, I'm still in awe that you're even coming. I love you.

To my brother Rob: I sometimes wonder how our lives would have turned out had we never been separated. It's almost ridiculous to me when people chalk up everything in life to coincidence. It is no coincidence that I ended up in Atlanta. I think you and I both know that. I am proud of the job you have done as a man, father, and husband; even though neither of us really had a glaring example of how to successfully do any of those things. You know I have your back…always. I love you.

To my brother Keith: I realize you're the quiet type, so we don't talk as much as we probably should. I hope I have been a good brother to you. If anything PLEASE learn from my mistakes. In the eyes of the law, you're an adult. But there's more to being a man than age. When you walk that line, I think you'll understand me better. Anyway, I love you.

To The Matriarch: Mom, all I've ever wanted for you is happiness. You haven't lived the life I think you deserve. But I'll do my best to change that until I die. That was my promise to you, and I intend to keep it. You have done all you know to do as a mother. You've made sacrifice after sacrifice for me. I can never truly repay you for that. Often we clash because I know you don't really understand me. But really, I'm nothing more than the strong man you raised me to be. I treat my wife so well because you taught me to respect women. I take care of her so well because I wish someone had done that for you. I have a purpose and a mission. I have to live that mission. Please understand that whether or not I agree with everything you say, my love for you is never in question. I love you.

To my father: I must admit that years ago I would have taken this opportunity to tell the world the many ways in which I feel you have failed as a father; but that's not who I am anymore. Sure there are things that could've been done differently, but that's all over now. As a man, I look at our relationship, or lack thereof, through a man's eyes. I now know what it feels like to have a child. I know what it's like to pay child support. I know now how hard it can be to understand my mother. I know how hard it can be sometimes to understand the decisions of your wife and or children. But I get it done, all of it. No one could make me do otherwise. In some ways, you and I are just different. But I can also recognize many of your characteristics within myself. To some degree, I am less critical of you. But in some ways, I am more critical. I don't know what our relationship will be like when one of us dies. I do however suspect it won't be any more than it is right now. But please understand that if nothing else, your blood is my blood. That is something that will not change.

oul:

'o "The Great I Am": Most people don't understand who you are and what you ant from us. I cannot say I always know either. What I do know is that I'm oing your work, whether some people recognize or like it or not. It is with your reath that I breathe. Thank you.

To my ancestors: I know I haven't done anything alone. So for all that came efore me so that I could walk with such ease, I thank you. You did not live and ie in vain.

Heart:

A quick shout out goes to all the kids at North Carolina A&T State University. If could have afforded to stay there, I would've been an A&T graduate. Big up ric, Terry, and Dave! In my heart, I'm an Aggie for life! (No offense, Ohio tate.) Keep your heads up young Black students, and don't let anyone tell you ou're "missing out" by going to a Black school. Aggie Pride!

To all my kids at AIM Education: As much as some of you can be irritating at imes, I don't have to tell any of you how much I love you all. I won't call names pecifically, because then I'd have to call way too many names. I wake up and vork because of you. Always remember what I've taught you, or at least most of t. Grow up and make some money! Thanks South DeKalb for believing in AIM.

To ATL: You're my new home and family. Atlanta really is the Black Mecca. All anyone has to do is visit awhile, and they'll see that. Now that I live here, I would never want to live anywhere else. I love you Eastside! No place in America has more to offer a Black man. Let's not waste our opportunities Black Atlanta. We can do this together. I love you ATL!

This book is for all my people in Akron, Ohio. Please know that in everything I do, I represent you. I see you working. Big Tone and John, you guys are family to me, and I'll always have your backs. Thank you to everybody who's ever believed in me. Thanks coach T.K. for putting me in the game. I love you Akron, and way to represent, LeBron! O.H.Ten for life!

Introduction

Many of us in Black America have grown comfortable. We've grown comfortable because on the surface we seem to have accomplished so much. Perhaps we have accomplished much; but while many of us smile, most of us suffer. Even those of us to who seem to live "The American Dream" are not truly in control of our own destinies. We've sought control through consumerism rather than power, and consumerism is easily given. Power has to be taken. 44 Questions for Black America is not only a series of questions, but also a series of answers. The real question is whether or not we as Black Americans are ready to hear the truth about us, by us. Please keep in mind that whether you like it or not, rest assured it is for us.

The Questions—

1. Why do we call each other "nigga"?

2. Why do we accept, commonly use, and glorify the word and profession "pimp"?

3. Why do we think light skinned people look better than dark skinned people?

4. What is "acting white"?

5. What is a Black American's role in Politics?

6. Why do we have bad credit?

7. Why do sisters have bad attitudes?

8. Why do we glorify drug selling?

9. Why are so many of our men in prison?

10. Why do our girls get pregnant so young?

11. Why is a fatherless household so common?

12. Why do our women degrade themselves in music videos?

13. Why are we proud to be called a thug?

14. Why do we think smoking weed is okay?

15. Why can't we work together to own businesses like other races?

16. Why do we give and get such poor customer service?

17. Why are we overweight?

18. Why do brothers date white girls?

19. Why do rappers and athletes keep acting like they're not responsible?

20. Why do we call our women "bitches" and "hoes"?

21. Why don't we pay child support?

22. Why don't we just educate our own kids?

23. Why do we think so much has changed in America?

24. Why do we have more AIDS cases than any other race?

25. Why don't we save money?

26. Why are we so critical of pastors and churches?

27. Why is straight hair considered good hair?

28. Why do we celebrate Dr. King, but not Malcolm X?

29. Why are radio stations allowed to play such inappropriate songs?

30. Why can't Black women get along with each other?

31. Why does the ghetto have to be violent?

32. Why are all the Black men on TV athletes, entertainers, criminals, or all of the above?

33. Why do we expect whites to treat us so well when we were once legally considered their property?

34. Why are our kids ashamed to be smart?

35. Why do we have to wear name-brand clothes?

36. Has integration helped us, or hurt us?

37. Why can't we be on time?

38. Why are so many of us unemployed?

9. Should Black Americans join the military?

0. What is the true "Black religion"?

1. Why are liquor stores only in "ethnic" neighborhoods?

2. Why don't police treat us fairly?

3. Why don't fathers have any rights?

4. Why can't we work together as Black people?

Answer to Question 1:

It's time Black America recognizes the difference between "nigger" and "nigga". *Nigger* is by definition, a negative adjective not specific to Black Americans. *Nigga* is a slang term that is commonly used as a simple pronoun. The hip-hop community has long since known the difference between the two. Perhaps Q-Tip put it best when he described the term *nigga* as, "a term of endearment".

The problem is that much of Black America confuses and associates the term *nigga* with *nigger*. In truth, *nigga* is in fact a derivative of the word *nigger*, and we obviously associate the term *nigger* with slavery. White Supremacists and "regular" white folks alike still use this term in a purposefully derogatory manner. Even if one does accept that there is a distinction between the two words, the line is thin, and fades quickly. When Jennifer Lopez used the word *nigga* in a song with Ja-Rule, a lot of Black people were outraged. The fact that she's Hispanic, which America considers as ethnic, helped her cause. Furthermore, she was on the song with a Black artist who incidentally thought it was okay. But even the coolest white boy might just catch a beat-down for saying "What's up, my nigga?" to his Black friend.

Most everyone agrees that the word *nigger* is unacceptable. But what about the word *nigga*? In an ideal world, we would be able to use one's intent to determine whether *nigga* is appropriate or not. The white girl would be able to say things like, "Y'all niggas talk too much!", and we'd know it wasn't racially motivated. But is that realistic? Unfortunately, this is an issue we'll likely continue to approach without logic, because it's somewhat illogical to embrace even a derivative of such a hurtful word. But *nigga* isn't going anywhere, and as long as you don't add that pesky "er", you're apparently okay. That is, of course, if you're Black. Whether they like it or not, white people will never be able to use *nigger* or *nigga*. Is the use of either word within Black America a good thing? Probably not; but there are certainly more pressing issues.

Answer to Question 2:

He's an unlikely hero, and one would assume, an even less-likely role model. With his brilliant furs, feathered hats, bright colors, gaudy gold chains, and alligator shoes, he surveys the block. With hawk-like eyes, he patrols the streets in his great big fancy car. Though he sometimes wears a cape, he isn't the "Caped Crusader". Rather than rescue them, he actually puts women in harms way, although safety is one of his selling points. He's a pimp, and we love him.

Is this some sort of resurgence of blaxploitation film genre? Or are we truly that hard up for someone to look up to? By definition, a pimp is someone who solicits the services of prostitutes and commandeers the profits. The world of pimps and prostitutes is far from the light-hearted affair the media portrays it to be. Many prostitutes begin walking the streets before the age of sixteen. Some were raped and molested as children, and as a result, lack the ability to manage their own sexuality. Some are runaways who simply ran out of options. But most are drug addicts clinging to their craft in an effort to sustain their deadly habit. Though they may have different stories the constants are often confusion, fear, and hopelessness. It is these conditions on which the pimp preys. His hoes brave sub-freezing city streets, exposing themselves to sexually transmitted diseases. Meanwhile, he gathers adoration as he rhythmically walks, leaning slightly on his exquisitely detailed pimp cane. While we admire his jewel encrusted "pimp cups", and full-length minks, a Sister pays for said items by selling pleasure from whichever orifice her client prefers.

How did a pimp become positive? Why has the media embraced pimps so? How can popular TV shows use the word "pimp" in their titles? How can actual pimps get cameos in music videos and movies? How can middle school students run around talking about how they're going to "pimp these hoes"? There comes a time when we have to exercise common sense. Pimps are not to be admired. It's not a game. It's a very real profession with very real consequences. Somewhere tonight, a mother will be bent over behind an alleyway dumpster and ferociously penetrated for $20. Somebody's sister will give oral sex to ten strangers in two hours. Tomorrow morning, someone's aunt will be found dead, murdered by one of her tricks. This harsh reality is a far cry from the diamond pinky rings and suede interiors we commonly associate with our urban heroes, otherwise known as pimps.

Answer to Question 3:

Years ago, a slave owner by the name of William Lynch spoke at a slave-owners seminar of sorts. The goal of this function was to implement practices that would enhance and ensure the prosperity of slavery in America. Among the proposed strategies was the use of skin color. The best slaves are not controlled by force, but by their own minds. Lynch suggested pitting the lighter skinned slaves against the darker skinned slaves. The plan was simple. You keep the dark skinned slaves in the fields and assign them hard labor. You give them pitiful, yet sufficient rations, and very meager sleeping accommodations. These would be your field-niggers. On the contrary, you keep the light skinned slaves closer to you. You give them jobs indoors, saving them from the heat and back breaking work their darker counterparts endure. You give them better accommodations, and you could even feed them table scraps. These would be your house-niggers. The darker slaves would envy the lighter slaves, and envy breeds animosity. If the dark slaves plan to escape, the light slaves who fear sharing the discomforts of the dark slaves, will warn the slave-master. This clear separation and favoritism towards lighter skin creates both conscious and subconscious psychological associations. Light skin or white skin becomes associated with favor, comfort, and rewards. Dark skin becomes associated with pain and suffering. Lynch promised that if implemented, these techniques would cause slaves to eventually enslave themselves, and that they would be slaves for hundreds of years. Lynch was right.

The dementia continued throughout our history in the U.S. as some Blacks discovered their ability to "pass", or be mistaken as white. Slave-masters commonly raped slaves, resulting in biracial babies. Sometimes, a biracial child looks white without close examination. Thus, said individuals would afford themselves certain opportunities not extended to their clearly Black Brothers and Sisters. Mothers would encourage daughters to marry lighter skinned gentleman in efforts to "lighten up" the family. Believe it or not, this attitude is fairly common today. You know who you are, the people who want "pretty babies".

Thinking back on my childhood, I can't tell you how many times we used the term "Black" as an insult. You didn't want to play outside too long because you might get too Black. A few brown skinned girls got attention, but not if they were too dark. We didn't think a girl was really attractive unless she looked almost half-white (we especially liked her if she actually was). Although we wouldn't readily admit it at the time, these attitudes continued throughout high school, and beyond. Even when we did like a darker skinned girl, it was usually her body we were impressed with, and not her dark face. It wasn't any better for the dark skinned brothers like myself either. It's only been recently that the dark skinned Black man is in style. But the light skinned brother is and always has been popular.

We have to question ourselves about what we truly believe. It's great to say Black is Black. But do we really believe it? More importantly, do we show that we believe it? We are dealing with a negative mentality that has existed for years. Consequently, the end will not be met overnight. Whether we accept it or not, words are powerful. Especially when received by children. We cannot continue to use the description of Black in negative ways. We must accept that the perception of beauty we have was predetermined by the dominant culture of the United States, which is unfortunately not our own. As such, we often subconsciously ssociate beauty with characteristics specific to whites. We've got to re-educate ourselves so that we can discover the true beauty that Black people possess, even though our media rarely reinforces it. True it may be difficult, but if we cannot find a way, we are contributing to Willie Lynch's cause.

Answer to Question 4:

t's the brother who says, "Dude; that's awesome!" It's the sister who'd rather listen to heavy metal than rap. By definition, acting white is when any Black person displays behavior stereotypically reserved for whites. As Black Americans, we seem to have placed ourselves inside a box. Inside this box there is only enough room for things like broken English and hip-hop slang, athletics, entertainment, and style and fashion. But it gets more specific. Not only is proper English unnecessary, but it is apparently only appropriate and normal for whites. If you get caught using proper English as a Black American you had better be at work, talking to your white supervisor, or completing some school assignment. Otherwise, you run the risk of being accused of acting white by your Black peers. If you are Black, you should be athletic according to most Black Americans. But you can't play hockey or soccer, because that would be acting white. In fact, it wasn't until Tiger and the Williams sisters that you could get away with playing golf and tennis. Even though Black Americans created Rock and Roll, listening to it is somehow acting white. Of course you have to wear the hottest hip-hop fashions, or you know what you might be called. But why is it like this?

Actually, the cause of the response itself is not illogical. Black Americans have developed an almost innate disliking for white American culture, and it's not at all necessary to explain why. As such, there's nothing worse than one of your own imitating the people who have caused you so much pain. The problem is that for whatever reason, Black America refuses to accept its diversity.

For the most part, when we're talking about someone acting white we're really referring to cultural traits, and not racial traits. True, there are certain cases such as a Brother or Sister wearing blue contact lenses in which one could easily be accused of mimicking the white race. But issues such as clothes, music, recreation, and language are social issues. Where I grew up in Northeastern Ohio, we coined the phrase "sell-out" and applied it to any Black person who seemed to have a white dialect. But we failed to recognize or care that not all Black people grew up the way we did. Many Black Americans grow up in predominantly white neighborhoods, go to predominantly white schools, and most of their friends are white. As such, they'll be exposed to a culture quite different from a Black American growing up in an all-Black neighborhood. It is this white-exposed Black

American that often has difficulty finding acceptance with his own. Yet it is his ability to understand and even relate to America's dominant culture that may give him an advantage in the business world and other professional arenas. For some, this reality complicates matters even more, as it breeds a sort of natural jealousy of which most "traditional-background" Black Americans will never admit exists. Such envy typically manifests itself in negative ways; hence the term acting white.

Jealousy Theory aside, most Black Americans are certainly not jealous of Black Americans they perceive to be acting white. Most Black Americans simply do not wish to identify with white Americans in any way; at least not when we don't have to. Unfortunately for the victims of "acting white" accusations, no one seems to care that displaying certain behavior isn't always intentional. These individuals aren't trying to sound white; that's just how they speak. It's how they've heard others communicate; possibly family, friends, and other people important to their lives. Things like the music you listen to, the clothes you wear, or the way you find recreation are products of your immediate environment. Just because someone doesn't sound like they belong on BET doesn't mean they wish they were white. Clearly certain cultural characteristics are associated with certain races. But in America, the cultural lines often cross. We must be careful to make the distinction between culture and race. The bottom line here is a matter of respect. Not being able to respect someone who speaks, acts, or lives differently than you do is not only childish; it is the very basis of racism.

Answer to Question 5:

We'll never forget the 2000 Presidential Election. We weren't at war, and the economy was good. Truth be told, if a president could serve more than two terms, there would've been no need for an election that year. But alas, Clinton was required to vacate his post. All Al Gore had to do was ride the coat tails of the prosperous U.S. economy Clinton had become credited with. Unwisely, Gore chose to distance himself from Clinton because of the "Monica" scandal. This was an event, mind you, that had absolutely nothing to do with Clinton's proficiency as a president. Black Americans were fearful of a Republican office, and even more frightened of the leadership of a seemingly incompetent son of a former President. We showered the polls like a monsoon, and there was a sense of urgency in Black America not seen since the Civil Rights Era. That fateful election night, many of us received the education of a lifetime.

The U.S. uses a critically flawed Electoral College System. In the Electoral College System, every state is assigned a certain number of electors based on poplation. The minimum any state can receive is three electors. In the Electoral College System, if a candidate could just win the 12 largest states, he'd win the election! In most elections, certain states become somewhat irrelevant. Technically, your vote only matters at the state level anyway. If the majority of people in your state vote for Candidate B, all of the electoral votes go to Candidate B. But perhaps the most disturbing flaw in The Electoral College System is the fact that electors are not obligated to cast a vote reflecting the majority. In other words, Candidate B could win the majority of votes in a state, and the electors could still choose to vote for Candidate A. Bottom line is, the Candidate with the most votes doesn't necessarily win the election. This was the case in 2000. But the most disturbing reality guaranteed by the Electoral College system concerns the power of the Black vote. Black celebrities regularly profess the power of the Black voters. But is there any real validity to this claim? The fact of the matter is that unless a candidate is able to secure fifty percent or close to fifty percent of the white vote, the Black vote is somewhat irrelevant. Examine the numbers behind this logic, and you'll find that Black Americans make up slightly more than 12% of the U.S. population. One might assume this 12% to be considerably influential. However, the allocation of this 12% is a critical factor. Black populations are typically concentrated. This dilutes our voting strength in the Electoral College system. States like Georgia for instance, have a highly Black concentrated Fulton County, but the majority of the state is white. Once the "Black voter's candidate" loses Georgia, all those Black votes become null and void. This type of scenario will continue to hinder the voting power of Black Americans unless America moves to a Popular Vote System.

In addition to the harsh reality of The Electoral College System, we also learned that an election can be stolen. Millions of Americans watched as Florida was "mistakenly" reported a victory for Gore, news that would have sealed the election for the former Vice President. But with George W's brother presiding as Governor, Florida produced a magic trick that would have made Whodini jealous. After the election, news surfaces that misleading ballots confused thousands of voters, and thousands of Democratic votes were tossed out for various reasons. Although undeniably valid, our complaints fell upon deaf ears. When numerous Black politicians couldn't get one single Senator to sign off on their formal political protest, Black America's objections became inconsequential. What message did the 2000 Election send to Black America?

The 2004 Presidential Election brought to light a more complex depiction of the Black American political structure. Black America is experiencing a political shift. A once faithful Democratic crowd, the Black vote is now up for grabs due to socioeconomic diversity, and traditional moral values. A segment of Black Americans have seen substantial economic gains over the years, and those who haven't have caught enough of a glimpse to see it as a feasible reality. Consequently, concerns such as tax relief for the upper-income bracket have moved more and more Black Americans to "relate" to Republican viewpoints. These days you are more likely to find a Black American wanting less government involvement than you would have thirty years ago, as Affirmative Action-like concepts are becoming unpopular in today's Black America. But perhaps an even bigger issue has been the Republican Party's ability to play on our moral convictions. This was blatantly evident in the 2004 Election, as many Black Americans were unwilling to separate church and state. Black religious leaders urged their congregations to cast their votes for Bush. Rather than focus on more pressing matters such as unemployment and a self-serving, misguided war, some of us foolishly shifted our attention to gay marriage, abortion, and prayer in public school. I watched and listened as proud-hearted Black Christians supported Bush, justifying said support with The Holy Bible. But the Bible says "Judge not lest ye also be judged". Scripture aside, we need to accept that satisfying the terms of the Constitution requires certain concessions. Otherwise, someone would at some point lose his or her freedom of choice. We must learn to recognize when we are confronted with unnecessary legislation such as bans on gay marriage, a ban on abortion, and a ban on prayer in school. A simple matter of choice can address such issues, with little to no infringement on the rights of others. If you're not gay, why are you worrying about gay marriages? If you don't believe in abortion, don't have one. If you really want to pray in school, why not just pray silently? Or better yet, go to a private Christian school. Whether or not you believe moral convictions should play a role in politics, it is clear that they do. Morality has ripped apart the once unified voting thread of Black America, as the Democrats struggle to make everyone happy by denying any liberal concepts when it seems convenient. In the end, this civil fracture spells doom for the voting power of Black Americans as a group, but suggests intriguing possibilities for both the Republican and Democratic parties. However, neither of the parties has courted Black Americans with much urgency, or effort for that matter. The Democrats assume we'll vote their way as we traditionally have, and the Republicans could hardly show less interest in winning our allegiance. Yet the Republican Party's ability to align itself with conservative "Christian" values is more than effective enough.

Whether we vote Donkey or Elephant, our condition as Black Americans changes little. Consequently, it's hard to believe in a system that never seems to work for you. Traditionally, Black America's involvement in politics has been limited to the receiving end. America's "stay in your place politics" is responsible for Black America's lack of interest and confidence in U. S. Government. Nevertheless, it is our responsibility as citizens to understand how our government operates so as to protect our interests. In a capitalist environment like ours, the real movers and shakers either have money or legislative power. A fortunate few, like the people who run for President, enjoy both. The average Congress member is a white male with above average income and education. Senators and Representatives are usually businessmen or attorneys, and don't depend on their six-figure government salaries to survive. These are the individuals that drive our political structure. So logic suggests our strategy as Black citizens should not focus on voting, rather acquiring more financial power.

More important than policy is the money that backs it. Come election time, most of Black America's issues surround economics. Even those that are not specifically economic issues, like education, are certainly affected by it. So why not attack the problem at it its source? It may sound cliché, but money sure as hell does make the world go around. Most of the tax cuts and government programs we are often concerned with have little to no effect on the wealthy. Rather than putting our faith in the political process, we should be channeling our energies into replacing government-funded programs with programs privately funded within our own communities.

Although voting should not be our focus, it is certainly a necessity. Voting is particularly effective at the local level where every vote is more likely to count. If for no other reason, we should vote out of respect for those who sacrificed so much to afford us the opportunity. If voting is not at least symbolically important, whites wouldn't have fought so desperately to keep us from doing it.

If we don't vote, it is easier for politicians to justify failing to implement policies that benefit us. Would you cater your campaign to meet the needs of a demographic that won't show up at the polls anyway? Politicians support those who support them. But becoming politically active once every four years is simply not enough. We have to find ways to impact our immediate communities whether it is an election year or not; hence the grassroots approach. So maybe you can't vote on an environmental bill. But you can certainly bend over and pick up a piece of trash from your street. You can discourage drug dealers and liqour-store owners from setting up shop in your neighborhood. We can even provide our own businesses, banks, and schools. We have to learn how to get what we want and need from our country whether or not the guy we voted for is in office. Politics is a year-round competition. Maybe it's time we learned how to better play the game.

Answer to Question 6:

Credit is without a shadow of a doubt, one of the most effective modern means of enforcing discrimination. Americans have both willingly and unwillingly succumb to a lifestyle dependent upon our ability to spend money we don't really have. Credit, in all its treachery, conceals itself as a tool of freedom. But it binds most of us. As Black citizens, credit is perhaps our biggest foe.

It all starts with the Evil Empire. Some call them credit bureaus. They've earned such an unfavorable nickname because of their blatantly deceptive nature. They present themselves as trustworthy, government entities. They would have you to believe that they are the protectors of your personal records. Many would argue that what they do borders on invasion of privacy. The bureaus would contend that they only receive information from companies who have extended you credit, and that all they do is compile that information. This is technically true. But writing your personal credit resume is a huge responsibility; one that should come along with more regulation than exists. Most people will have at least one mistake on their credit report by at least one bureau. These mistakes can keep you from getting the things you want, like a car or a home. Credit bureaus make it clear that their job is to compile reports, not deal with people. The phone numbers they give to the general public won't get you to a real, live person. In fact, you typically have to write them (often more than once) just to get a phone number that will get you to a human being. They will usually attempt to discourage you first before they actually try to help you, and they will do anything to avoid an actual conversation. If you can get past a few roadblocks, you'll actually be able to contest inaccurate information. Credit bureaus are obligated to "investigate" any dispute within 30 days, or they have to remove the item from your report. Guess what "investigate" means to them? This means someone from the bureau will call the creditor and ask if the debt is valid. Now the creditor wants money, and has no incentive to clear you, especially if it's a collection agency. If they say the debt is valid, that's the end of story. That's also the end of the "investigation". The credit bureau won't even call the original debtor once something gets to collections. They couldn't care less what happens to you and your credit. They don't get paid to help people.

What credit bureaus do get paid for is your personal record. They take a look at your credit habits and history, and they assign you a number. This number is known as your FICO score, and in America, it's worth more than its weight in gold. If you are above 620 or so, you are probably okay. If you are under 600, you become a victim. The lower your score, the harder it is to get credit, and the more verything costs you. Companies will pay top dollar to find out who can make hem rich. The more they know about you, the less risk they feel they will take. Not only do the credit bureaus charge companies wishing to extend credit; they harge **you** for **your** own history. How fundamentally wrong is that? To add to heir list of dictator qualities, the government won't allow you to sue a credit oureau for making a mistake! As if all that isn't enough, the general public does not know precisely how credit is scored. We have an idea of what helps and hurts, out there is no published, consistent, guaranteed formula. If the bureaus were required to divulge the system of FICO score calculations, then citizens would be able to spot discrimination. Maybe that's why they are not divulged? How can the government allow something that affects us so tremendously to be determined in secrecy? But come to think of it, the government does that all the time.

So where does discrimination come into play? The bureaus contend that a oureau employee has no way of knowing one's ethnic affiliation. But certainly there are relatively race-specific names. For instance, you'd assume a guy named Leroy Watson to be Black (or any girl whose name phonetically makes no sense). You'd assume Jose Ramirez to be Hispanic. Kim Li is probably Asian, and it's a good bet that anyone with the last name of Goldstein could be Jewish. Names aside, once someone has access to your social security number, they can find out just about anything about you. But the real discrimination likely begins outside of the bureaus, and within the entities that buy your credit history. The bank may tell you that your credit score determines whether or not you get a loan. But even the bank will admit there are other factors. What are these other factors? Based on our history in the U.S., are we really supposed to be naive enough to think race is never a factor? Need I remind you that they used to make us know the number of bubbles in a bar of soap in order to vote? How do I know that a person with a lower score than me didn't get approved for the same loan I was refused? The bottom line is that people extend credit; not the computers the people often blame once you've been denied. People are imperfect. People play favorites. People are racist. Since the majority of individuals extending credit are White, these facts become problems for Black America.

Although discrimination is a legitimate factor, it is not necessarily the biggest factor. For the most part, our credit problems are the result of the culture we as Black Americans have accepted for ourselves. No other culture is as superficially identified as Black America. Everything we are is based on what we have. Speaking as a representative of the hip-hop generation, all we really want is designer clothing, a couple of luxury cars on custom rims, and a big house with a huge flat-screen plasma television. In all honesty, the desires of the generations ahead and behind mine are not much different. Now I certainly am not against fine living. You can't take it with you, so why not? But this philosophy only applies to those who truly can afford such a lifestyle. Black Americans often seem to miss this key element, and credit supports this tragic mishap. With credit, you can look like a million bucks, even if you never make a million in your entire lifetime. Herein lies the problem. The credit industry preys on Black Americans because it is fully aware of our extrinsically focused affliction. But we are hardly victims as we willingly toss ourselves into debt for the sake of our lavish desires. All of these things, so many of which we can't really afford, are conveniently placed just within our grasp. Most people will make the minimum payments. Although this keeps you in good graces with your creditor, it will take you a lifetime to pay the balance off by making minimum payments. Nonetheless, you do it anyway because it's affordable, until you lose your job or have a couple of unexpected bills. Your grace period passes by, then a month, and then another month. Before you know it, you're afraid to answer your phone because some #!*hole is on the other end acting as if it's <u>his</u> money you owe. Your life is now filled with a constant barrage of attempts to badger you into paying money you obviously don't have. In the eyes of the credit world you are now a risk, and your credit score and dignity pay the price.

So what do we do as Black Americans? Now I won't even fool myself into believing that we'll just stop using credit. For some of us, it's our only means of survival. But we can strengthen our chances of getting credit by having more Black lenders. Theoretically, a Black lender is more likely to see beyond our skin color and see us as a worthwhile investment. Besides idealistic philosophy, and perhaps a more likely motivation, Black lenders could profit from a market that is both poorly served and under-served. Our current predicament is one in which non-Black companies exploit the Black consumer, blaming credit as justification for ridiculous interest rates. The bottom line is that because we often have fewer options, lenders are not always willing to be flexible (or reasonable, for that matter).

The best choice is to not depend on credit at all. What ever happened to cash? Our desires for expensive clothes, cars, and cribs have all but eliminated this once useful method of payment for most people. We refuse to accept that luxury cars are for the rich, and that "rich" may not describe our financial state. With credit, we can probably get it anyway, even if we have to work two jobs to pay for it. Everyone dreams of being rich. But think about what it would be like if you didn't have a mortgage, rent, or a car note. What if you didn't have credit card bills? You could work at a fast-food restaurant and feel rich if you didn't have all

ose bills. What if you only bought things you actually had cash for? Credit
ould ideally be reserved for your home and emergencies. If you can live by that
andard, you'll be a lot better off. At that point, who cares what your credit score
?

nswer to question 7:

ost of us would love to say that this is just a stereotype, but we just have too
uch supporting evidence. In all honesty, this is obviously a generalization and
oes not apply to all Black women; but it applies to enough of them.

Perhaps we should first define "attitude" (as if that's necessary). We've all seen
he snake-like head and neck movements, the waving of the fingers, and the
ands on the hips. Attitude also includes but is not limited to "getting someone
old", "reading someone", "rolling the eyes", or a good old-fashioned "cussing
ut". Is this some sort of instinctive response, or is it environmental?

In our country, the media often plays the role of deity, parent, friend, and so
many other roles it should not. For the most part, the media tells us who we are,
and we believe it. Are little Black girls born with bad attitudes, or is that something they saw on T.V.? Is a bad attitude something they learned from a big sis-
er, or cousin? How about a parent, or neighbor? Most of what children learn is
he result of what they see others do. In terms of the media, much of this whole
"attitude" issue may have begun with the Blaxploitation Film Era. For the first
time, Blacks could beat up on whites in film and get away with it. Once the white
movie producers realized just how badly we'd want to see that, they quickly saturated the movie market with these types of films. We paid to see Black people
standing up for themselves; something we could rarely see in the real world. Pio-
neers like Pam Grier showed a strong, confident, sassy, and outspoken Sister.
Such a Sister became somewhat of an idealistic role model. As society evolved, so
did the Sister; and she brought a little "Foxy Brown" with her. But a simple
reflection of confidence and independence has been manipulated and trans-
formed into a bad attitude. The Black woman represents not one, but two minorities; and we all know what the media does to minorities. Much like the Black
"thug", the media has hand crafted the "Bad Attitude Black Woman". In reality,
people become who they are expected to be. Why do you think so many Black
young men want to be rappers or athletes?

Not only is having a bad attitude seemingly acceptable; it is often expected of
Black women. As Black Americans, it is our obligation to dispel such myths. The
modern Black American woman is in fact confident, but she exhibits courtesy,
grace, and a refined sense of self-respect. Sisters often excel in the business world;

an industry in which having a great personality is vital. Maybe some Sisters do have a bit of a chip on their shoulder. But think about what they've had to endure. They've been used, abused, raped, and oppressed by men both Black and white. They get paid less than any other race/gender specific demographic group even when doing the exact same jobs as men do. Come to think of it, it's amazing that all Sisters don't have bad attitudes. The bottom line is we must accept responsibility for creating our own identities. If we keep letting others write the script for us, we can't complain when they don't write in a happy ending.

Answer to question 8:

It almost seems cliché to blame the music, but you have to call a spade a spade. Just about every hot rap album includes some references to drug selling. The inevitable consequences: prison-time and or death, are overshadowed by the "street-credibility" gained. Even the rappers who profess to live the finest life styles claim they had plenty of drug money before they were rap stars. It's almost as if a rapper's resume has to list drug sales as previous employment in order for anyone to take him seriously. Even if it is true, which it often is not, why would one broadcast criminal activity?

As much as we would like to blame all our problems on rap music, the fact remains that the music is to some degree, a reflection of the society it represents. Drug dealers are popular in the recording studio because they are popular in the streets. Why wouldn't a kid in the projects admire the local dealer with money to burn? Let's see: bus-pass, or Benz? Flip burgers for a week and make $200, or make $200 on the corner in an hour? Sure there's the risk of death or prison. But a kid in the ghetto may risk these things anyway. The police are going to harass you just because you're a young Black male; and you certainly don't have to be doing anything wrong to catch a bullet. Without those pesky W-2 forms, you don't pay taxes. Plus you can get the best looking women, because women like nice things. You don't have to wake up early, and you can pretty much make your own hours. To top it all off, people fear and respect you. Sure you are destroying your own community. But it's been destroyed for years. The drug-game is recession-proof. In fact, it's probably the only industry that actually improves during times of recession; and it will never stop because there will always be "fiends". It's easy for one to rationalize that addicts will get drugs from someone, and that someone might as well be you. Although selling drugs is fundamentally negative, it isn't necessarily irrational.

What legal options are available to a young Black male struggling to make it? Even the minimum wage jobs are disappearing in our joke of an economy. If you're relatively poor, your educational resources are often insufficient, thus eliminating even more of the few meager choices you had to begin with. So what is one to do? You can't pay rent with morality, and you certainly cannot eat it.

Those of us who have taken the time to investigate know that our drug issue in Black America is by U.S. Government design. Drug selling is meant to be appealing, as well as destructive. But it was never intended to escape the ghetto. The drug problems in the suburbs are as, if not more serious than in the inner city. Like any other temptation, it's about your conscience and what you can deal with. Most of us could never stomach the risks of drug sale, or the negative impact it has on any community. But for those who can, it will remain a lucrative career choice.

The keys to solving this problem are educating our youth and providing more employment options. The higher the level of education you have, the more likely you are to be employed. Better yet, an educated person is more likely to become an entrepreneur. With the U.S. failing to protect its citizens from overseas employment, the Average Joe is left jobless.

Though we can fight it, drug sale isn't a problem that is likely to disappear anytime soon, if at all. There's a lot of money to be made in illegal narcotics, and I'm not talking about the guy on the street corner. The real *ballers* are the ones who seemingly have legitimate income. The 14 year-old on the corner doesn't have the money or resources to ship drugs overseas. If white America would acknowledge the true dynamic of the drug game, there'd be a whole new meaning to the phrase "sleeping with the enemy". Such an acknowledgement would likely implicate several important figures, and would demand serious changes in America's "war against drugs". One could argue that ideas such as these carry conspiracy theorist undertones. But you have to ask yourself why a country that spends billions on technology, weaponry, and surveillance would have such a hard time keeping drugs out. What most Americans will never accept is the fairly obvious fact that America and many of its business associates profit from drug sale. We accuse the Middle East of using illegal drugs to fund their military campaigns, yet we support them by buying their oil. Let us not forget that Bin Laden is just a disgruntled ex-employee of the United States. Columbia grows the coca plant, but they buy the chemicals necessary to turn it into cocaine from us. It is primarily money, not safety that dictates the decisions our government officials make. Take tobacco for example. Cigarettes are far more dangerous than most illegal narcotics, regularly cause more death, and are proven to be as addictive or more addictive than most illegal drugs. In fact, cigarette companies are required to print the fact that cigarettes are unhealthy right on the label. Yet no one is even debating banning cigarettes. Losing the profits from Sin Taxes, the unusually high taxes on tobacco and alcoholic products, is apparently not worth saving lives.

The drug war is a war best fought one community at a time, and would require the individual members of that community to be on one accord. It would require everyone to agree that drugs simply will not be tolerated, and everyone would have to be willing to risk their own personal safety to guarantee that. Most importantly, they would also have to be willing to deny themselves the potentially large sums of "blood-money" the occupation brings. In the end, this is where the war is being lost.

Answer to Question 9:

When examining most of the issues facing Black America, the causes are usually a combination of "us" and "them". The issue of the Black man and incarceration is certainly no exception. At last tally, Black Americans make up 43.7% of the nation's prison system. This from a group that only makes up a little over 12% of the entire U.S. population. So what about "them"? For most Black Americans, the question isn't whether or not we are targets, rather why. Conspiracy Theorists would contend that our rate of incarceration is a part of White America's ploy to destroy the Black Race. The overall concept of a genocidal agenda may seem unrealistic, but let us not forget the Holocaust. As absurd as it may seem to some, the goal of a Blackless America isn't necessarily that far from the truth; at least not the origin of it all. Once it became more difficult to legally exploit us after the Civil War, White America saw us as competition rather than free labor. In a capitalist society, one succeeds by either outperforming or eliminating the competition. Hence the assumption of genocide. Although White America's original intention may have been to remove us, it would seem that at some point the strategy became to just move us. White America doesn't want to destroy us, but it's clear they don't want to live next door to us. We as Black Americans support this economy. Where many Black Americans feel we have advanced because most of us make more money now than we have in the past, the less naive Black American recognizes the truth. The truth is that we're big spenders. By race, Black Americans spend the highest percentage of our income. If we don't get good jobs, we can't buy White America's expensive and often unnecessary products and services. Now this is not to discredit the accomplishments of Black America. But White America has no less domination over our economy than they ever have. If they truly wanted to lock us out, they could do it pretty easily. The point of all his is White America doesn't want to destroy us. They do however want to beat s, and locking us up is a great strategy.

Being mistreated by the legal system somewhat comes along with being Black. eople would like to pretend that the racist sheriffs that spent nights burning our omes and hanging us have all died off. Although people die, ideas do not. Like nergy, ideas are not destroyed, only transferred. People are no less racist today han they were a brief 40 years ago during the Civil Rights Era. If people are still acist, this means we still have racist cops, district attorneys, judges, and other eople of power in the criminal justice world. No intelligent human could xclude this as a contributing factor to the unnaturally high incarceration rate of he Black male. Take Wisconsin for example. Wisconsin has a Black population f 6%. Yet Black prisoners total 48% of the prison population. Maryland has a rison population that is 77% Black! But the Black population of the state is only 28%! This type of disparity is consistent throughout the country.

As usual, the media makes its mark. The Black Male has been America's text-book villain. Any crime committed can easily be blamed on the Black male, and few will question. Television is sure to show that even our Black role models are susceptible to leading lives of crime. The Black man is America's worst night-mare. He's dark, different, and often physically superior. Despite blatant racism and concealed discrimination, the Black American man has achieved prolific accomplishments. But jealousy breeds hate, and hate has turned the Black man into a villain. What do we do with villains? If television has taught us anything, it's that we either kill or lock up the villain, and the hero rides off into the sunset. The image our media has created is so strong that the average American, Black or white, would describe the typical criminal as a Black man. Television is just as responsible for racial profiling as the police departments that teach it as manda-tory practice. Popular television shows have made millions reinforcing this image. Some intentionally, because a Black man is about the scariest thing you can be in America.

Injustice aside, we must still accept some responsibility, perhaps the bulk of it. If a bear walks into a hidden trap and is caught, the bear is a victim. But if the bear knows the trap is there and still gets caught, you'd have to question the bear's intelligence. The regularly discriminatory behavior arrogantly displayed by our country's legal system should make us leery, if not paranoid. When it comes to Black America and Criminal Justice, the word *justice* is optional.

Black America's dissatisfaction with The Justice System is not limited to wrongful convictions. More prevalent is disproportionate sentencing. White Americans regularly receive lighter sentencing than do Black Americans. In the case of cocaine for example, it would appear that even legislation supports these practices. Cocaine is a drug more commonly used by white abusers than Black ones. It is relatively expensive, and is often the drug of choice for celebrities and highly paid professionals alike. Crack, which is a derivative of cocaine, is more commonly used by minorities because it is less expensive. Yet even though cocaine is more expensive, it carries a far lighter sentence than does crack. Even the smallest infractions committed by Black Americans will not necessarily be treated as small.

The U.S. Justice Department found that 28% of Black men will be sent to jail or imprisoned in their lifetimes. Yet the fact still remains that the majority of incarcerated males are not unjustly imprisoned. Many of us **do** engage in illegal activity, and this is what we must address first. From a fundamental standpoint poverty begets crime. By improving education in our communities and encouraging Black-owned enterprise, we can begin to alleviate some of the frustration clearly evident in Black America. Now this is not to say that the conditions leading to deviant behavior have not been engineered with the intentions of incarceration. To some degree, our challenges exist by design. But that all becomes irrelevant at trial time. The playing field is not even; we need to recognize, but not accept that, and then make adjustments. We cannot effectively "point the finger" until we've first done all we can to limit crime within our communities.

Answer to question 10:

What was once a family embarrassment has now become all too common. "Babies having babies" is the infamous phrase plaguing our communities. But why does it happen, and what can we do about it?

We have to examine physiology as a factor. Medical studies show that on average, Black girls become sexually mature sooner than do their Caucasian counterparts. Is this a valid explanation as to why Black girls get pregnant sooner? In terms of the nature of humans, visual stimulation is key to reproduction. If a man sees certain body parts with a certain "look" seen in a certain way, the man will become aroused. This arousal prepares him for sexual intercourse. Other factors such as increased blood flow to sexual areas can also encourage sexual activity. A girl who is sexually mature doesn't only look different, but she'll likely feel different. The girl is now more likely to become sexually stimulated than she was before puberty. Once a female can technically carry a baby, she's at risk for pregnancy.

In all fairness, the numbers in this particular issue are not necessarily as telling as one might think. Statistics show that Black girls have babies sooner than White

irls. But the real issue is not so much the birth, but the pregnancy itself. Statis-
cs would leave one to believe that Black girls must be having sex younger and
ore frequently. This data however is difficult to fairly assess because in most
ases, it is dependent upon students admitting to those acts. It is unlikely that
here is as much difference between the sexual habits of Black and white teens as
ost data would suggest. One of the biggest problems with statistical data per-
aining to teen pregnancy is that it cannot adequately gather the number of abor-
ions. It is possible that young white girls get pregnant just as often as Black girls
o. The difference may be that white girls are having more abortions.

Money affects everything, even teenage pregnancy. In terms of the above men-
ioned abortion issue, it is as simple as being able to afford the procedure. Sure an
dult can see that it is far more expensive to keep a baby than to get the abortion.
The reality is that none of that matters when you just don't have the $300. There
re government programs to help young mothers. There are no government programs that will pay for an abortion. But the biggest issue Black Americans have
with abortion isn't money, rather morality. Abortion is one of the few topics for
which our typically Democratic population turns Conservative Republican. The
majority of Black Americans are Christians, and Christians are unmistakably pro-
ife. As such, abortion isn't an option for many pregnant Black teens.

Black girls are more likely to have a single parent home environment. This
elays to the likelihood that while that one parent is at work, the daughter is
ome alone. This obviously applies to male teens as well, and allows more time
or uninterrupted conception. When polled, teens cited time alone as the most
nfluential factor as to whether or not they become sexually active. Teens can be
ikened to sexually hormonal volcanoes waiting to erupt. Regularly leaving them
alone is like leaving a starving dog alone in a room full of steaks. I have the pleasure of working with teens on a regular basis. Trust me when I say that parents
haven't got a clue. We'd love to believe that our children are the sweet, innocent
youths we remember. But once a child hits puberty, his or her parents also need
to undergo a transformation. Teens have these adult desires and relatively adult
bodies, but a child's ability to make decisions. This can be quite a dangerous
combination in terms of sexuality. As a parent, it is best to assume your child is at
least considering becoming sexually active so that you can take proper measures
to discourage such activity. But so commonly, parents are either naïve or in
denial about just how grown up their little angels are.

One of our biggest problems is Black America's social dynamic. The aforementioned time alone is critical. This becomes more complex when you combine
it with the responsibility of the Black father. When polled, Black women who

had given birth as teens felt that if their fathers had been more involved, or involved at all, their pregnancies would have never occurred. Speaking as a male approaching a female with a father present is different than when there is no father. A father implies a certain threat of physical danger, which means a suitor will approach the young lady with a greater amount of caution and respect. When polled, young Black males said that they were more likely to go to a girl's house later at night if there was no father present. They also said that they were less likely to do things such as sneaking in or bringing the girl back home late if there is a father around. Unfortunately for single Black moms, a man apparently demands more respect than does a woman when it comes to young Black males. A single mother may need to be a bit stricter. She may not pose the same psychological threat, but she can be just as effective by consistently enforcing certain rules. Also, maintaining a verbally open relationship is critical, especially in the case of same-gender parent-child relationships. A parent who encourages open discussion about sex is more likely to have a positive influence on the child's decisions concerning sexual promiscuity. Talking sex with your child may seem uncomfortable and awkward, but it's worth it.

One of the reasons young girls get pregnant is because they don't know how to respond to a male's affections. Young girls without an active father will sometimes crave attention. They'll get that attention at some point, but where it comes from and how they get it may be problems. The easiest way to get attention from a high school boy is to "give it up". If the young female finds pleasure in sexual intercourse, as she often does not as much as one might think, she can easily justify a decision to become sexually active. What she was looking for was attention. She just wanted the boy to like her, or "love" her, in teenage terminology. But as adults, we all know how that goes. All she typically gets is a bad reputation, a disease, a baby, or some combination of the three. A father can reduce the chances of his daughter getting pregnant early by regularly showing her affection. If a father can show his daughter that he loves her, and is interested in her, she won't be so easily impressed with a young boy trying to get into her pants. A father has to talk to his daughter about things that are important to her and show a genuine interest in her life. Also, a girl needs to see appropriate male-female interaction. She needs to see her father open doors for her and her mother. She needs to hear her father tell her mother sweet things and buy her simple gifts for no apparent reason. She needs to see her father treat her mother with respect. All these things are going to form her expectations of a man.

There has been debate over the issue of handing out condoms to kids. Actions like this follow a philosophy that it is a response to the inevitable. "Kids are going

:o do it, so they should at least be safe." But opposition believes that handing out condoms is really just encouragement. It's almost like saying, "We expect you to do this, and it's okay." Hence the issue of community acceptance. A sixteen year-old pregnant girl is no longer the shame of the neighborhood. It's not a big deal at all anymore. I recently visited Miami, and found a high school that actually had a day care facility for students with children. Such programs certainly help teen mothers, but do they encourage teen pregnancy? This question cannot be answered at the conceptual level, rather on an individual basis. For some, the fear of pregnancy or sexually transmitted diseases is enough to keep them from having unprotected sex. If they feel that a condom will protect them from said outcomes, then acquiring a prophylactic may in fact give a teen the go ahead. But more than likely, a teen assumes that things like pregnancy or HIV only happen to *other* people. Teens wanting to have sex will do so whether a condom is available or not. As such, providing teens with condoms is worth risking the rare case in which it might encourage an otherwise abstinent teen to have sex. However, programs such as day care in high schools don't deserve the precious tax dollars they absorb, especially since there are more pressing needs that effect all students and not just students who are parents.

There are three things parents need to do in order to help prevent teenage pregnancy. First of all, we have to let our young Black girls know how important they are. They have to respect and love themselves enough to avoid sexual encounters. We cannot be with them 100% of the time. So at some point, we have to have confidence in a child's ability to make a good decision. Much of that child's ability will depend on how good a job we have done as parents. They have to get love and attention from parents, so they don't go looking for it elsewhere. The stronger the bond between a girl and her parents, the less likely that girl is to become pregnant.

Secondly, we have to stop placing all the blame on our young Black girls and start focusing on our young Black boys. After all, these pregnancies aren't possible without them. Contrary to most opinions, mine is that the greatest responsibility in limiting teen pregnancy falls on the shoulders of our Black American boys. The teenage culture is no different today than it ever has been. In terms of sexual promiscuity, the male drives the culture. Typically, a teenage girl has sex because it's what the teenage boy wants. When asked whether or not they felt sex was necessary in a relationship, the majority of boys answered "yes", and the majority of girls answered "no". This would indicate that it is boys that dictate sexual activity. Our focus is often placed on young females because they bear the pregnancy, the child, and typically most or all of financial responsibility for that child. The male can simply deny the child is his, and go on with his life. Along with popular culture, Black Americans almost encourage promiscuity in teenage boys. We are more likely to ignore our knowledge of a son having sex, and condemn it when we find out our daughters are doing it. This "boys will be boys" mentality is blatantly evident in the music our Black teens listen to. We have to start taking the same protective approach with our Black American males as we do with our females. This is far more effective than assuming a teenage girl filled with erratic emotions and unfamiliar feelings can ward off an aggressive young man who has society's "green light".

Thirdly, we just have to make conception as difficult as possible. Limit unnecessary private time. A teenage girl will likely want to spend a lot of time alone. That's fine, as long as she's truly alone. Do your best to know where your kids are, especially on overnight trips. When polled, most teens confessed that they commonly had sex in their own homes while parents were at work. This is difficult to combat, but it would be in your best interest to find a solution such as an extracurricular program. My research found that the biggest contributor to Black teen pregnancy is just too much free, unsupervised time. No matter how much you may trust your teen, you just can't make a habit of leaving them alone. That's the bottom line.

Answer to Question 11:

As if the Black Man hasn't taken enough heat, we must address the issue of the M.I.A. Black father. First off, by no means am I implying that there aren't any good Black fathers; I'd like to think I'm one myself. But there is a problem.

The saying "Age ain't nothin' but a number" is not the case when it comes to fatherhood. On average, Black American fathers are younger than Caucasian fathers. A young father is less likely to be ready for the responsibilities of fatherhood. It may be clever for us to say, "If you're old enough to make one, you're old enough to raise one", but it sure isn't accurate. How great of a father can a sixteen-year-old really be? Should we even expect things to turn out well? Most teens haven't even "found themselves" yet. According to the law, anyone under 18 is a minor. This means they aren't completely responsible for themselves, let alone someone else.

Young age is a part of another problem we have in Black America. Every year, a substantial amount of Black children are born to an unwed mother. By no means does this guarantee disaster, but it does increase the likelihood of the mother raising the child alone. Although over half of all marriages end in divorce, divorcees often have a chance to bond with a child before the separation occurs.

n many single-parent situations the child is, for lack of a better word, a mistake. n this predicament, the independent nature of the Black Woman plays a vital ole. Most Sisters would rather raise their child alone than beg the father to be nvolved. A man that really isn't interested in raising an unplanned child doesn't need a whole lot to walk away.

The Black Woman rarely needs help doing things all by herself. But the government's aid doesn't hurt. It may be unintentional, but our government discourages the family structure. Think about this scenario. You're an 18-year-old girl, and you just had a baby. You're not married, and the father makes less than $20,000 per year with no medical benefits. Now you could get married, and struggle to survive. But why try? If you both work, you'll have to pay for childcare. But an unmarried mother can qualify for heavily discounted or free childcare. Without a degree, and limited work experience, you and your husband would have low paying jobs. You'd barely make enough to buy diapers. But if you don't work at all, you can get money and food stamps. Besides, minimum wage jobs don't typically have benefits. What happens when your child gets sick? You can't do better than government benefits, especially for free. The type of housing you and your husband could afford will likely be unsafe, unsanitary, and unsightly. But an unwed mother can qualify for low-income housing and stay in the same quality home as most working couples, at a fraction of the cost. Oh, and if you get married, you won't get child support. When examining these such issues, it's easy to see why a young mother would opt to stay single.

The bottom line is that the mind of the Black father has to change. We have to be better, not just for our own children, but to be examples to young men. To do this, we must first educate ourselves. We, as a community, must understand what it truly means to be a father.

Being a father has four components:

- Financial responsibility

- Quality time

- Genuine interest

- Development

Financial responsibility is an aspect that has unfortunately become misused and misunderstood. For some Sisters, it's all about the child support. Although one could argue that financial support isn't necessarily the most important responsibility a father has, it is certainly necessary. Simply put, a kid has needs and you can't buy diapers with good intentions. Since the beginning of time, man's responsibility to his family has been to provide.

Quality time may sound cliché, but quality time is the best way to describe what type of time a father needs to spend with a child. Quality time is best defined as time you spend with your child in which he or she has your undivided attention. Think about it. How many of us actually do that on a regular basis?

Most parents have done it. The child tells us something that honestly seems uninteresting, but we pretend to be so excited. Sooner or later, parents have to show genuine interest. Fathers often have trouble doing this with daughters. It's easy to get into your son's football game, but what about a dance recital. Some times a father will only find interest in the fact that his child is happy. Although this isn't ideal, it's certainly good for the child.

Development is what it's all about. Children look to fathers to see how to become an adult. They'll mimic most of what you say and do. The type of adult they turn out to be is largely dependent upon what type of father you are.

P.S.—I didn't forget about you, single moms.

It's impossible for a mother to be both mother and father, even though I know several moms who've come close. A family has two parents by design, and it was never really meant to be optional. Now you can't just introduce any and everyone into your child's life. But if you can find a male role model that you can trust, it sure doesn't hurt. Don't overlook organizations like athletic teams, churches, and clubs. As a teen, I often would watch the men in my church to see how they interacted with their families. I'd watch the Black attorneys and businessmen, and try to imitate their countenance. Athletes and entertainers are fun to love, but children need real-life, everyday role models. They need to interact with a father figure, or at least a positive Black male. But in the end, all you can do as a single mother is the best you can. You may know better than anyone what a good man should be like. Remember that just because they don't have a great father, doesn't mean they can't grow up to be one.

Answer to question 12:

If ever there was a time better judgement should supercede freedom of choice, this is the time. The degradation of the Black woman brings new meaning to: "Forgive them Father, for they know not what they do." Is it really necessary for a up video to be filled with half-naked women in order to spark interest? It's an undeniable fact that sex sells, but at what cost?

The cost, in this case, is respect. Although what we see on television is not accurately reflective of the Black woman, it's often difficult to convince the youth of that. What's more dangerous is the fact that young girls imitate this behavior. Eleven and twelve year-olds are just itching to get to the club and display Nature's gifts. So if the girls seem to think it's okay, and the boys are reacting to a combination of natural biology and learned behavior, who's to stop this thing from getting worse? Activists and concerned sisters everywhere say **they** will. But they haven't yet found a way to match the omnipotence of the music and television industries. Furthermore, the way in which they choose to protest is often misguided. Rather than attack the parent companies and labels, they tend to attack the artist. The responsibility should at least be shared between the two. Besides, energy is better used when focused on the positive rather than the negative. A more productive approach is to provide young sisters with better examples of what being a woman is all about.

Women bear most of the burden in the issue of Black Women's portrayal. But it's the same old industry challenge. If you say no, there's always someone else who'll say yes. Besides that, entry to the entertainment world is narrow for sisters, so sometimes you've got to get in where you fit in. But alas, when does morality matter? Is it okay to pretend to be a hoe, as long as you aren't one for real? Is dancing provocatively on camera justified if it's "work"? If you ask the video models, a.k.a. video hoes, you'll get a resounding, "Yes!" Number one: These are grown women making grown decisions. Some would consider the manner in which most video girls are portrayed to be exploitative. But since no one is forcing these women to do anything, it's difficult to view them as victims. Number two: Viewers still have the responsibility of separating fantasy from reality. Videos are filled with provocative, gorgeous women because in real life, it's highly unlikely that you'd ever see that many beautiful women in a club doing the things the video girls are doing. If videos showed commonly realistic images, no one would really want to watch them. Number three: You don't pay their bills, so you really can't tell them what to do.

Whether we want to accept it or not, Sisters dressing and acting inappropriately is no different from "gangsta rap". It's entertaining to some, but it does cause problems in our communities. The solution to this problem, assuming you think it is a problem, lies within individual families. It is the responsibility of parents and other positive adults to instill whatever values they see fit. We have to approach problems like this one girl at a time. At some point, all of us will have to accept responsibility for the state of Black America, even if that means forego ing some of our sinful pleasures. That is, at least in public.

Answer to question 13:

These days, being labeled a thug is a compliment, or at least acceptable. But what exactly is a thug by today's standards? Surprisingly, it's pretty much defined in the same way it has always been: a common criminal.

A thug, for whatever reason, chooses to live an illegal lifestyle. It's assumed he always carries at least one firearm, and isn't afraid to use it. He is likely in and out of jail, and is willing to do whatever it takes to survive. No matter what, a true thug <u>never</u> fills out W-2 forms, unless he's washing his money with a record label or barber shop. Your modern thug has sex appeal, and several hip-hop icons sell the thug image. He's a more hardened, rough around the edges Black man, complete with scars, stab-wounds, and bullet entries. Many sisters would even contend that thugs are better lovers. They're assumed to be rougher, take-charge types of guys. A thug can be easily identified by his appearance. He might have gold teeth, a gang scarf, and tattoos with violent themes (you know, like R.I.P. bullets, guns, knives, etc.) As for the clothing, the pants will typically be jeans (khakis on the West Coast). The top could be anything from a plain white tee shirt, to a throwback jersey, or a hooded sweatshirt so you can hide your identity as you commit crimes. Of course, you can find said attire in your run of the mill rap video. This is because the thug-look unfortunately doubles as the standard hip-hop look, and kids who aren't really thugs are often misjudged.

So where did this come from? Like much of our current culture, it is derived from hip-hop. Hip-hop is the Black urban-based culture that began thriving in the early eighties. Much of it involves rap music. But hip-hop is a culture, and music is only a part of any culture. The culture of hip-hop was initially a voice, a way for urban Black youths to speak to the rest of the world. Through the years, it has been corrupted, distorted, misrepresented, misused, and misunderstood by marketing and White America. Nevertheless, hip-hop still tells the story of the streets. Thugs are part of that story. Poverty often leads to and creates crime. As a result, the thug is born. It's nothing new, but no other culture admires thugs the way we do as Blacks.

They say you can either do what you love, or love what you do. In our case, it seems we have chosen the latter. The thug life isn't a reality for everyone; not even some of the self-proclaimed thug-rappers. Kids listen, watch, and imitate. Isn't that how kids are designed to work? If they didn't work that way, they'd never learn anything. So now you have these quiet suburb kids carrying guns, seeking violence, and convincing themselves they're thugs. Some legitimately are. The saddest part about all of this is that we've accepted it. Not only do we accept it; we sell it, ignoring the consequences as we so often do.

Cultivating a society in which thugs are admired is completely illogical. So how do we stop it? The answer isn't as simple as banning rap videos that encourage violence, although that may not be a bad idea. The root of the problem is within our Black American communities. Real thugs are born to real frustration. The more legal income opportunities we provide for ourselves, the fewer thugs we'll have.

Answer to question 14:

It's almost a joke to say marijuana is illegal, when in fact, it is. Smoking weed is about as common as smoking cigarettes. Musicians make regular references to "Mary Jane", and the metaphors they use are gradually becoming less creative, *if* they use a metaphor at all. The question is whether or not it is okay to smoke weed.

Let's just pretend that there is such a thing as "medical marijuana" for discussion's sake. Besides that, what are the benefits? The consensus seems to be relaxation, as is the case with most mind-altering agents. But the general public is unaware of the risks of marijuana. From a fundamental standpoint, regular smoke inhalation of any kind is damaging to your lungs. Also, there is the commonly known side effect of memory loss to consider. But the most concerning effect of marijuana is its effect on the human immune system. For those needing to brush up in Biology, the immune system is your body's defense against bacteria and viruses. Marijuana weakens your immune system, which makes it easier for you to get sick. This makes us more susceptible to AIDS, and Black America already leads the nation in the number of AIDS cases per year.

There are also legal ramifications to consider concerning marijuana. It seems all too common to see a famous Black athlete or entertainer arrested for possession, not to mention the regular Brother on the corner. True, it's less dangerous than cigarettes. True, the only reason it's illegal is because the government can't tax it. But how can we in good conscience encourage a habit that is addictive, harmful to the lungs, damaging to the immune system, and illegal? At some point we've just got to use common sense, or at least moderation.

Answer to question 15:

This is going to sound a bit racist, so my apologies in advance. But it pains me to go out into my own community and see that everyone owns something in it but

us. The corner-store owners are Arab, Korean, Indian, or something I can't identify. The major stores are usually white-owned. Here and there you'll see something Black owned. But the percentage of Black citizens is almost always higher
than the percentage of Black business-owners. Enough is enough! What's going
on?

One thing that usually isn't going on is capital. It's not necessarily the case
that Black people are not motivated, creative, or qualified. Our biggest deterrent
is usually money. Any significant business will typically need a minimum of
$10,000 to get off to a reasonable start. Most people don't have that type of cash.
So in comes the loan. Now as we've explored earlier in this book, the credit
industry is perhaps the most effectively racist industry in the United States.
Numbers don't lie. If you do get a loan, you'll probably be required to put down
much needed cash, and your interest rate will be so high that it'll be years before
you can turn a profit. But then how do foreigners get their loans? The common
misconception is that the U.S. government is giving them loans. But that's not
really what's happening. Foreigners often have their own banks. It's not the type
of bank we're used to, just more of a fund primarily available to people of a specific ethnic background. They have their own networks of ethnicity, which can
provide capital. When a foreign gentleman is turned down for a loan by a U.S.
bank, he can still get money from a group of individuals who share his ethnic
background. This way, he can be more fairly evaluated as to whether or not he is
a risk. Black America has no such network. There's no reason why we couldn't,
but we don't. Part of the problem is that we don't trust each other. Unfortunately, that lack of trust is often justified.

Black Americans are no strangers to obstacles. In fact, obstacles make up much
of our history here in America. Gaining capital can be difficult, but certainly not
impossible. It will likely just take more time, patience, and planning, than most
of us would anticipate. But the thing that is perhaps the most critical to the success of any business is sacrifice. We often hear jokes about how ten Mexicans will
live in a one-bedroom apartment, or how seven of them will pack into a tiny car
on the way to work. But behind most stereotypes, there lies a bit of truth. Most
foreign owned businesses rely on family participation and a unified goal in order
to survive. Go to the average beauty supply store, and you'll find that the staff
members are likely related. In the beginning of such businesses, just about everyone is underpaid, if paid at all, and overworked. But it's this type of work ethic
and sacrifice that eventually propels them to success. Next thing you know, that
family owns two stores, then three, and so on. Are we as Black Americans willing
to make such sacrifices? There are individuals who are willing, but they usually

ren't in a position to make a sacrifice because they have too many bills to pay. If Black Americans are to truly compete in the business world, we must first design our lives in such a way that saving money is a priority. This means limiting necessary expenses, and eliminating those that are unnecessary. Being a successful Black American business-owner includes factors far too numerous to cover quickly. But our focus has to be financial, because in business, money is the bottom line.

Answer to question 16:

If there are 10 employees working at the time you enter your neighborhood grocery store, why is only one line open? The line is clearly backed up, but yet the employees seem to have more pressing duties like straightening items on the shelves, or moving random boxes. If you ask someone for help, you might get it, but you'll also get some sucking of teeth, or maybe even a deep exhale coupled with a rolling of the eyes. No one seems to know basic things like store policies and procedures, and the one person who does know these things is always off that day, or on a break. Why do employees make you feel like you're bothering them when you simply call upon them to do their jobs? Why do employees not understand that they shouldn't use the work-phone for personal calls, and that they could at least hang up when a customer comes in? Most importantly, why do these problems so regularly occur in Black America?

Black Americans sometimes have a servitude complex. Anything that remotely resembles slavery is subconsciously resisted. What separates servitude from slavery is compensation. But in many cases, the compensation is not significant enough for us to commit to the servitude. Rather than find another employer, most individuals will keep the job, under-perform, and consistently complain. Consequently, the consumers pay the price.

Another problem is just a simple lack of good old-fashioned home training. In terms of showing respect and using proper manners, the expectations we place on our Black American youths are too low. They shouldn't have to be trained to say Sir, Ma'am, please, or thank you. But much of etiquette begins with pride, and the youth of today's Black America find no dignity in customer service. Most could benefit from a simple examination of the term "customer service". It means that you serve customers; it's not that difficult. Many of us are eager to be the boss so we can walk around with our heads high. But we don't realize that in order to be the boss someday, we might have to clean a few toilets first. Humility is a trait rarely seen in Black America because it is so often forced upon us.

In all fairness, it's difficult to find comfort in servitude when you were first introduced to the country as slaves. Furthermore, for years we were legally limited to service positions. As such, it's sometimes impossible to tell whether it is your lack of qualifications, or your skin color that keeps you from getting the job you want. A mentality such as this makes it challenging to emit the selfless exuberance necessary for good customer service.

The bottom line is that once you put on the uniform, all these issues become no more than excuses. As a community, the only way we can put an end to poor customer service is to demand better. If you don't like something an employee did, tell them about it, and what you want them to do about it. If you don't get the results you want, go to their supervisor. Keep working your way up the chain of command until you are satisfied. Don't be afraid to call the corporate office. That phone number is usually easy to find. If all else fails, stop giving them your business and encourage others to do the same. Remember that any business has to make money, and a business can only make money for so long with unhappy customers. You are important to them, and they know it. But if we don't exercise our right to be satisfied, then we concede our power.

Answer to question 17:

By now, we all know that Americans are the fattest people in the world. Much of this is reflective of our wealth. So to some degree, it's an honor. But within this statistic, there lies a harsher reality for Black Americans. By percentage, Black Americans are more likely to be overweight than White Americans are. Why is this?

Compared to other cultures, Black Americans are less likely to find fault with a few extra pounds. A lot of Brothers, especially in the South, prefer a *thicker* woman. Whereas a five-foot, seven-inch white woman weighing 180lbs may have trouble getting a date, a Sister with the same dimensions will likely have no trouble at all. Now of course there are other factors in this comparison, such the actual distribution of that weight. The joke has always been that White women have no butts. Black American women on the other hand, have gained a reputation for having relatively large backsides. To put it bluntly, Brothers typically don't mind a Sister being a little overweight, as long as the weight is in the right places. Brothers just want curves. In addition to what we like, our genetics play a role in our weight. As Black Americans, our African heritage typically yields a higher density of mass, and we tend to be larger overall than Caucasians. America has also left its genetic mark. When slave-owners would have us to boil their vegetables, they would leave us with the water the vegetables were boiled in as soup or our meals. What they didn't realize is that all of the nutrients had been extracted in the boiling process, and we were getting all of the vegetables' benefits. Due to the combination of nutritional benefits and a laborious lifestyle, slave children were often larger than white children were. Both the African and American contributions are evident today, as seen in our domination of sports.

For the most part, we as Black Americans have accepted our weight problems. We've been so consistently criticized in our history in the U.S., that we teach our children to respect and love themselves no matter what. This is one of the many beauties of Black America. It encourages a Sister who is fifty pounds overweight to walk with her head high, as she should.

The problem with the "Fat and Lovin' It" concept is that there are health risks associated with obesity. Like most humans, Black Americans are overweight primarily because of the foods we eat. Traditional soul food is high in fat, high in salt, high in cholesterol, and often uses pork, even if just for seasoning. We ate chitterlings and hog-head cheese because those are the parts of the pig that whites didn't want. Embracing it as necessity is one thing, but continuing to eat it as a staple when clearly healthier choices are available is another. Oh and for the record, everything doesn't have to be fried. But let's be real. It's that same unhealthy fat, salt, and pork that makes the food so delicious. I wouldn't even pretend to believe that baked chicken tastes better than fried chicken. Good taste is hard to argue with.

A particular sector of Black Americans struggles with diet for a different reason. Some Black Americans live in areas where there are no large grocery stores. They survive on corner stores for daily sustenance. The problem with this is that there will hardly be any fresh fruits or vegetables, if any at all. Almost all the food will be processed, packaged, or canned. This means the foods are loaded with additives, preservatives, sugars, and salts. The fat content in such foods is high, while the nutritional value is low. Even those Black Americans who live in the suburbs still have grocer issues. I live in a predominantly Black suburban area. After visiting a white suburban area, I noticed a difference in grocery stores, even when it was the same franchise. The white suburban grocery stores have entire sections with organic foods, meat substitutes, and even healthy desserts. In my neighborhood, the health section is significantly smaller. Mind you, these stores both have the same name on the front. This leads one to ask, "Do they not sell it to us because they think we won't buy it, or is it because they don't think we deserve it?" We are the consumers, and if we want stores to sell healthier foods, we can get that. That's the power of the consumer!

Many of us have adopted a fast-paced lifestyle, and in a country where convenience is number-one, the fast food industry has been more than happy to accommodate us. It doesn't matter where you eat; just about all the major fast food chains are unhealthy if eaten on a regular basis. First of all, most of the food is pre-packaged. This means that harmful additives and preservatives are necessary in order to maintain a certain taste. Secondly, the most popular method of fast food preparation is frying because it is fast and inexpensive. However, frying is the least healthy means of food preparation. You wouldn't think it, but almost all fast foods have sugar, and you already know they are high in fat, cholesterol and salt. Even though the major chains now offer a few relatively healthy menu items, most people don't go to a burger joint to buy a salad and fresh fruit. Most Black Americans eat fast food on a regular basis, and we are certainly feeling the effects. What's worse is the effect it's having on our children. Black kids are now fatter than they ever have been. Some of this is because many of them just lay around the house and play video games all day. But a high-fat, unhealthy diet is most of the cause. Children naturally have a high metabolic rate, meaning they're designed to burn food quickly. This being said, it is unnatural for a child to be obese. Let's examine the average dietary day for the average Black American child. My research shows that for breakfast, most kids eat some sugary cereal. You know the types; they usually have a cartoon character on the box. As the kids got older, say age 12 or so, they were more likely to eat some sort of pastry, muffin, or doughnut for breakfast. As they get older, children tend to choose to sleep later rather than get up earlier to eat breakfast. So if they eat breakfast at all, which I found out many kids do not, they eat something they can quickly grab and take with them. Toaster pastries were very popular in my study, and after examining the contents I concluded that toaster pastries don't offer much health value. Doughnuts are perhaps the most fattening food, ounce for ounce, a child can eat for breakfast; and muffins are surprisingly high in fat, although they are marketed as a healthy food option. There is yet another group of Breakfast Kids. These are the kids that get a ride to school in the morning. On the way, the parent stops off at a fast food restaurant for breakfast on the go. In these cases, health is traded in for convenience, and a boatload of grease and sugar is thrown in to sweeten the deal. Lunch is yet another dietary opportunity for Black America's children to bring themselves closer to an early grave. The little pre-packaged lunches many of the elementary level students in my study took to school are insanely high in sodium. In fact, many daycare programs won't even allow students to eat them. The public school system does attempt to provide a healthy lunch in some cases. But they forfeit that effort by giving the students options. There are vending machines filled with soda, chips, cookies, cakes, and candies. What normal kid would choose green peas? Most of the high school students interviewed divulged that they ate a vegetable at lunch no more than twice per week, unless of course it was the lettuce or tomato on their sandwiches. A significant amount of female students cited salads as a relatively consistent choice. But once they described their meat-filled, cheese topped, high fat dressing doused creations, it became evident that any health value had been overridden. Dinner is commonly the only healthy meal of the day for many of Black America's children. It's typically the first time a parent gets a chance to cook. Most parents have intentions of providing a healthy diet for their families, but busy schedules sometimes supercede those intentions. The majority of students in my study cited eating fast food for dinner twice per week or more. I should note that delivery pizza was included as fast food, as it is not prepared in the home, and is fairly high in fat and cholesterol. Overall, it's fair to say that the typical Black American kid doesn't have the best diet. Technically speaking, their diets are generally too high in the fats, oils, and sweets group, and their ratio of carbohydrates to proteins is one which promotes obesity because of our next issue.

Regular exercise in Black Americans has decreased, and regular exercise is one of the main deterrents of obesity. This reality is particularly critical when it comes to our children. Video games and television combine to form many Black American youths' recreation. Gone are the days when children would stay outside and run and play all day. Our mother used to have to yell outside and make us come in. Now the kids are already inside playing on their video game systems. The parents aren't getting much exercise either. Although there are countless home-gym machines on the market, most people buy them and then hardly use them. Gym memberships are a common expense for many Black Americans. But just because you belong to a gym, doesn't mean you have the time or consistent motivation to go. Furthermore, a good portion of gym-goers have no real clue as to what they should be doing anyway.

If you are overweight and you really don't care, then more power to you. Most unhealthy foods do taste better than unhealthy foods. Butter, oils, fats, and sugars make food taste better. You know what they say: "You're going to die of something." But the bottom line is that being overweight can lead to health problems such as high cholesterol, high blood pressure, and hypertension to name a few. So for all of you who are dissatisfied with your body-fat content, here are some real, scientifically undeniable tips to help you lose and or control your weight. It's called **The Wilson Diet**.

- Don't eat any complex carbohydrates at dinner. This includes bread, rice, and pasta. Too much bread and pasta will keep your stomach plump.

- Don't eat past 7 p.m. The assumption is that most people will not go to bed before 10. Always leave 3 hours to burn food before you go to bed. Doing a low impact exercise like walking after your last meal is ideal. But don't do it too close to bedtime if you have a hard time sleeping. It might charge you up and make it difficult for you to get to sleep.

- Drink only water or 100% natural fruit juices. Try to drink at least a quart of water per day. No soda! If you drink milk, use skim milk or soymilk.

- Avoid fried foods. Using the grill is a tasty alternative.

- Use common sense. Stay away from cookies, snack cakes, and foods like these. No one has to tell you these foods are unhealthy in excess. It's okay to eat them from time to time, but the key is moderation. If you know you can't do that, then remove them altogether on certain days. Also keep in mind that you have to work those sweets off with exercise later.

- Eat 3 or more meals per day. These meals should be in 3-hour intervals. A good schedule might be to eat at 6, 9, noon, 3, and then 6. This will speed your metabolism, and your meals will consist of smaller quantities of food, making it easier on your body. If you don't eat regularly enough, your body will hold onto everything it gets.

- Limit your dairy products. Cheese is okay, but take it easy. Don't eat it unless your food will taste horrible without it.

- Exercise at least 3 days per week. Exercise has to be a part of your schedule, or you might not get to it. It can be as simple as walking one mile.

- Include some form of strength training. Building muscle burns fat. You'll lose fat quicker this way. You might find that you actually gain weight once you begin a weight-training program. This is because muscle has a higher density than fat. Pay more attention to the way your clothes fit than the scale.

- Reward yourself on Saturdays. Pick one day per week that you can eat whatever you want. Just make sure that it's always the same day, and that you can exercise that day and the day after.

Please understand that these are only tips. Although they are fundamentally sound, they cannot guarantee results. Consult your physician before beginning this or any diet program, as this diet may not be healthy for you.

Answer to question 18:

Well we know how the Sisters feel about it, at least when it comes to "broke" Brothers dating white women. Before proceeding, it is necessary to point out that the majority of Black man-white woman combos are strictly sexually motivated. Jungle Fever stricken couples will often meet in the bedroom rather than a crowded restaurant for dinner, as their public union all but guarantees embarrassment and discomfort. But on the issue of Black men and white women as a whole, Black America is divided. The majority of Black American men are still clearly against marrying outside of our own. But concerning dating, the lines become blurry, and when it comes to sexual relations there is barely a line at all.

The question is no longer about <u>how</u> Black America feels, but about how Black America <u>should</u> feel. In some cases, finding something in common with another person is more so socioeconomic. This is evident even with Black couples, as we tend to choose life-partners with economic backgrounds like our own. Theoretically, a Black man who grew up poor may find he has more in common with a white female who also grew up in poverty than he does with a Black female who grew up wealthy. Your overall perspective is often heavily influenced by your financial history. As such, how one lives his or her life becomes as, if not more important than race for some people. Much emphasis has been placed on the common example of wealthy Black male athletes dating and marrying white women. Professional athletes have expressed to me that as they move into a different financial bracket, they more regularly encounter white females on a social level. If said male is not necessarily making an effort to seek Black women, dating white women seems justifiably reasonable. Applying this type of justification to Black men overall operates under the assumption that a Black male dates Black women due to availability, and not because we share the same ethnicity. So the question now becomes: "Does it mean anything that a Sister is Black?" The answer is an emphatic "Yes". In many cases, a Brother dates outside of his race because he doesn't understand this. A Black woman is the most magnificent creature God ever created. No other ethnicity of woman demonstrates a more perfect balance of strength and grace. Most Black women are both confident and compassionate. They have endured the oppression of our nation, and have managed to walk proudly. White women spend millions on tanning, lip injections, and plastic surgery. All this is done in an attempt to mimic features most Black women have naturally. Their often full-figured bodies demand allegiance, and their minds are paralleled by few. But a man who is only in search of physical pleasure will undervalue the Black woman.

There are a few perceived differences in behavior between white and Black women. One belief is that white women are far more subservient than Black women are. It is nearly impossible to prove whether or not this generalization has any merit. But most of us could site examples in support of this belief. If this belief is true, in general of course, our history would logically have a lot to do with that. It's easier to be subservient when you've never had to be. From a Sister's point of view, it must be difficult to be subservient to the white man, and white woman, and then come home and be subservient to your Black husband. But the issue goes further, so as to address the perceived attitude difference between white and Black women. A lot of Brothers just don't want to deal with the attitude Sisters can sometimes carry. Even though any intelligent human knows that persons of any race can have a bad attitude, the perception is that Sisters have it more often than anyone else does. This is a perception of which I'd have to agree is unfortunately compelling at times. White women are perceived to be less confrontational. They seem less likely to be loud in public, or get someone told, or cause a scene. Many a Brother accepts these perceptions as fact, and therefore admires the relatively docile demeanor that in his mind, a white woman offers.

Another issue is sexuality. Brothers tend to believe that white women are more sexually liberated than Sisters are. In other words, they're freakier. The consensus is that white women are more likely to do things like having a threesome or giving oral sex. As such, it is most often curiosity that drives the Black man to explore relationships with women of Caucasian persuasion. He wonders whether or not she feels the same, whether certain parts look the same, or whether or not she does the same things in bed that a Sister does. The myths range from differences in vaginal odor, to the amount and consistency of vaginal moisture. In some cases, once their curious questions have been answered, the Black man resumes his normal dating preference of Black women. However in some cases, the Black man recognizes and appreciates the white woman's differences and includes her as a consistent sexual option.

As much as we may examine this issue, there is a far less complicated conclusion to draw. For some Black men, a white woman is just another woman. There is no hidden desire to possess what we once could not have, nor is there some repressed gratification in enjoying white-skinned, forbidden fruit. One might get the impression that Black men who date white women only want them for sex. But this is often not the case. For some Black American men, a white woman is another female. As such, he seeks to develop a relationship with an approach relatively identical to his approach of any other woman. This demographic is probaly larger than most give it credit, particularly in the younger generation of Black men. Such a utopian attitude is often good for the soul, until it runs into the brick wall that is American Society. I was raised as a Christian, and Christianity had always taught me that to deny someone based on the skin color is fundamentally wrong. After all, Jesus offers salvation to people from all nations. But as my understanding of religion versus spirituality grew and evolved, so too did my understanding of the reality of the United States. I have known several Caucasian women who, race aside, exhibited qualities that certainly would have made them relationship candidates. But life emits a sometimes unspoken, but sometimes spoken law that supercedes idealistic desire. For me, it isn't worth the dirty looks, being made into an outcast, or the imminent feelings of betrayal against your ancestry. Not to mention creating biracial children that will have trouble finding their place in a clearly racially divided country. The fact of the matter is that although it sometimes appears that southern separatist themes have subsided, white America is no less disgusted seeing its daughters in the arms of *coloreds*. Both parties in a biracial relationship are likely to become ostracized by their respective communities, in a "modern" society far less evolved than it claims to be. We label the Brother a sellout, and Caucasians dub the damsel a slut. But for many biracial couples, these challenges are outweighed by the joy and fulfillment love brings.

Fundamentally, it is important to any race that the males and females reproduce with each other in order to ensure the race continues to flourish. In my case, this task required no effort because I prefer Black women. When you consider that many of our Black American males are going to prison and leading violent lifestyles, it becomes more critical that those men who are not in said situations commit themselves to Black women. If nothing else, a Black man marrying a white woman could be viewed as somewhat disrespectful to the Black woman. Especially given that the ratio of women to men is more disproportionate in Black America than any ethnic group. There are so many available Black women that it seems almost ridiculous for a Black man to marry anyone else. Some of us have become so pro-integrate that we fail to recognize a need for exclusivity. We sometimes fail to properly maintain the balance between integration and preservation. Separation is not a bad word. Unfortunately, we as Black Americans find it hard to draw the line, even when white America clearly does it for us.

Answer to question 19:

Many an athlete has borrowed Charles Barkley's famous quote: "I am not a role model". Although his point is well taken, the reality is to the contrary. You can't

determine whether or not you are a role model. Others do that for you. Tha
being said, athletes and entertainers do have a certain amount of responsibility.

Everyone is human, which means everyone makes mistakes. People drink, d
drugs, beat their wives, get traffic-tickets, and just break the law in general. Bu
when these individuals are famous, there's another element to deal with. Impres
sionable minds are watching. True, everyone deserves to live without bein
judged, or without constantly being on display. But the money celebrities mak
seems to be a fair trade-off to most, as it is that same lack of privacy that make
celebrities household names.

How entertainers conduct themselves is more critical to Black Americans tha
to white Americans because Caucasians tend to provide their children with
broader array of wealthy people to look up to. When you see a white man drivin
a Bentley, what do you assume he does for a living? Most people might answe
occupations such as doctor, lawyer, stockbroker, or businessman. But if you see
Black man in that same Bentley, what would you guess he does for a living
Would you answer athlete, entertainer, or maybe drug dealer? The bottom line i
that people look up to people with money. Although there are numerous opportunities for Black Americans to make money, one would be led to believe tha
athletics and entertainment are our only legal options. Therefore, Black entertainers and athletes are role models whether they like it or not. Many athletes and
entertainers realize this. But there is a major difference between some of the
superstar athletes and entertainers of today and those of the past. Many of the
great athletes and entertainers of the past were able to transcend their professions
and leave a permanent, positive mark on society. The bold political statements of
the greatest Boston Celtic center ever, the Black fists of the 68 Olympics, and the
activist actions of a Public Enemy are now only memories in a celebrity culture
that is sometimes devoid of such leadership. Those modern athletes and entertainers who regularly profess Black pride often earn media punishment. Others
simply choose a less conspicuous approach. The modern Black celebrity is by no
means a slouch however, as some pour millions into special foundations and
community projects. But words can be stronger than donations, especially when
it comes to cultural change. Money can be beneficial to the success of any movement, but it runs out at some point. Words however can live from generation to
generation. The problem is that Today's athletes and entertainers need to be mar-
ketable if they are to truly capitalize on their status; and speaking up for Black
issues can be suicidal to one's image. As much as we claim to detest generaliza-
tions made about Black Americans, we ourselves often expect our famous to have

convictions they simply may not have. So perhaps there is no obligation here. But what is more tragic than an opportunity forfeited?

Despite public consensus, we cannot impose our expectations onto Black celebrities; nor should we. How one chooses to live his or her life is a personal decision. Rather than hope that a famous ball player or rapper sets a good example for your kids, why not be the role model yourself? Children's lives are most impacted by people they see and come in personal contact with on a regular basis, not someone they see on television. We shouldn't expect a millionaire quarterback to teach our young boys much more than how to throw a football, and to be honest, a regular father can do that too. During their teen years, it may seem as if you are the last person they'd ever want to be like. But in the end, your kids will depend on what you've taught them. Real role models don't have to be famous.

Answer to 20:

At its basis, this issue is similar to the use of the term *nigga*. To some degree, words like *bitch* and *hoe* have been softened. You can say *bitch* on almost any television station, when before it was outlawed. Much like *nigga*, *bitch* is often used as a term of endearment. For example, "I love Keisha. That's my *bitch*." However, both *bitch* and *hoe* carry negative connotations, and are typically used in an insulting manner. Afro-folklore insists that the last thing you can ever call a Sister is a *bitch*. In fact, it may literally be your last word.

These days, words like *bitch* and *hoe* are regularly substituted for *woman*. For example, "The *hoes* love it when I wear this shirt". More concerning than the blatant disrespect is the long-term effect associated with such behavior. The issue is not so much the words themselves as it is the devaluation of Black American women. Words do hurt, especially when passed from generation to generation. As time goes on and these words continue, the moral fiber of Black America erodes. We are descendants of The East, and Eastern Civilization holds senior women in high regard. Yet these days, ignorant Black teenagers call elderly Sisters *old bitches*. The Black woman is the cornerstone of Black America. She is not only called upon to attain her own success, but to support the Black man. Without her, there is no life. How can we even conceive mistreating her?

Such language is most commonly an issue in music. What we must realize about the music world is that although some pledge their allegiance to artistic expression, most pledge their allegiance to the almighty dollar. People say and do what sells. We as consumers control the sales. Need I say more about the solution?

The bottom line is that correction for this atrocity starts at home. We have to teach our young boys that Sisters are never to be addressed as bitches or hoes. We must also teach our young girls never to accept it. As for music; this world revolves around money. In America, people listen better with their pockets than they do with their ears.

Answer to 21:

Why don't some Brothers pay child support? Divorcees and baby-mamas all over the nation are trying to figure that one out. There are a few answers, although it somewhat seems irrelevant.

The most common answer is that some father's just don't care. There's no way to sugar coat it, although it can be difficult to fathom. For me, providing for my children is innate. It's more of a reflex than a choice. But some do not share such instinct. Maybe their father didn't do anything for them? But how is it truly possible not to care about your own child?

The simplest rationale can be found in the fact that many people don't care about themselves, much less another human. Although there is absolutely no excuse for failing to pay child support, there are some valid reasons that this occurs. A lot of it often has to do with the relationship between the father and the mother. In most states, the mother is Queen and King when it comes to custody. Much like being Black in America, a man has little chance for a fair trial in a custody battle. If the plaintiff and defendant were never married, the woman is pretty much going to get everything she wants unless the man can afford a high-priced attorney. Child support payments are determined based on income, and usually total around 20% of gross income. But in family law, child support payment calculations are about the only thing that is fair. Even though the calculations may be fair, there is no way for the man to determine how the money is being used. Often times child support payments are used from everything from cruises to expensive purses. A woman can use child support payments to buy a luxury car and justify it by saying that the child needs a safe car to ride in. Actually, the law doesn't require her to justify it at all. This reality can be frustrating to a man, especially if money is hard to come by for him.

Animosity between parents sometimes leads to the father's inability to detach his anger with the mother from his responsibilities to his child. In this case, it is the child who loses. A frustrated man wants to be "finished" with the woman who has changed his life, especially if he didn't want a child in the first place. This attitude, coupled with many Sisters' "Me and the baby will be fine without you" philosophy, often gives the father an out. Also, guilt isn't always an issue for athers. One man explained that when he found out his ex was pregnant, he asked her to have an abortion. He made it clear that he did not wish to be a father. When the woman decided to have the child anyway, he felt he was justified in completely removing himself from the situation.

Some men are just selfish. It's not more complicated than that for some fathers. That being said, it's best that women protect themselves. Sister's, when you're dating a man you even think you might become intimate with, ask him what he'd do if he got you pregnant. You'll probably catch him off guard, so you'll be able to tell whether or not his answer is truthful. Remember ladies, condoms break, and no method of contraception is 100%.

But what do you do if it's too late for all of that? Well the bottom line is that children are expensive. You didn't create that child alone, so you shouldn't pay for it alone. If necessary, the courts will have child support removed from the father's check and sent to you without him having to do anything. Don't allow your pride to take money away from your child. You may not really need the child support in order to survive, but it helps. Besides that, it is the father's obligation.

As a man who pays child support, I cannot relate to men who won't pay it. I've known men who won't work a legal job just so they can avoid child support. Supporting your child isn't a punishment; it's an honor. It's your responsibility—end of story. Maybe the child is too young to understand your selfish failures. Or maybe the mother doesn't want your child to know how poor a father you are, so she hides the truth for you. But if you don't pay your child support, how can you respect yourself? Regardless of how you feel about the mother, or even if you didn't want the child in the first place, you have to be a man about it. Even if you have fallen on hard times, do whatever you need to do to take care of your child. Otherwise, you're not truly a man at all, and Black America could do without you.

Answer to 22:

Make no mistake about it; Black America's students are behind. When compared to Caucasian students, Black students score lower on standardized tests, have a higher dropout rate, a lower graduation rate, and a lower percentage of students attending college. It's not that we're mentally inferior, so what's the problem?

One issue, though not the most important, is financial. Even at the college level, the average Black institution pales in comparison to most white schools. Such is the case at the high school, middle school, and elementary levels. The better your facilities are, the more resources for learning you are likely to have. Tax dollars in an upper class white county will yield quality white schools. This is no necessarily the case concerning Black schools however. Even in Atlanta, where the economic distance between Black and white is often slim to none, the difference in school facilities is still significant. This reality questions the allocation of tax dollars and other monetary issues such as the PTA, fundraising, and private funds. In the end, questions remain unanswered, and facilities remain unequal.

Statistics show a direct correlation between income level and academic performance, and facilities aren't the only factors. Black Americans are by percentage more likely to be poor than white Americans are. It's nice to say that poverty can't keep a child from being a good student. But in actuality, living in a low income situation can pose several obstacles. There is a certain mentality that exists among the poor that is not as common with the wealthy. A poor child has a survivor's spirit. He has little time to dream, as he must focus his energy on simply making it. My mother taught third grade students for 30 years; the majority of which lived in low to middle-class areas. She found that it is challenging to impress upon a student the importance of learning his spelling words when he doesn't know whether or not he's going to get dinner. A child living in poverty often has very adult-like responsibilities such as cooking, cleaning, and supervising siblings. Although these things may teach character, it is often detrimental to what they need to learn in school. Besides duty to family, a poor child typically has a completely different life perspective than a child who is financially secure. Education may be a remedy for poverty, but it is a long-term remedy, and the poor have immediate needs. Said needs often outweigh those of a potential future that isn't even guaranteed; even Maslow agrees. School doesn't offer a struggling elementary student any timely solutions, yet it attempts to convince him that school is somehow important. As educators, it is our responsibility to put students in a position to excel. We cannot motivate them; that has to come from within. But we can provide them with both encouragement and the proper learning tools. As if that alone isn't hard enough, an educator must master the art of making otherwise boring information seem interesting and exciting. Being a great educator of Black American children requires a combination of talent, desire, and proficiency that is often lacking in today's public school structure. This is because the training and monitoring necessary to consistently produce such teachers is a mystery to most school boards, and is therefore nonexistent.

"You have to see it to want to be it." It's hard to have aspirations of a legal, wealthy lifestyle when you don't know, or ever meet anyone who has done it. The ghetto has few such role models. The average child living in such a community will have difficulty establishing the relationship between academic success and nancial success. One of the reasons the ghetto is *the ghetto* is because it is mostly filled with individuals qualified for low-skilled labor. Opportunities for low-skilled labor have all but vanished in this country. The persons who most benefit from education are the professionals, of which the ghetto has few.

Many people misunderstand the purpose of school integration. It wasn't our desire to learn along side whites that led us to push for an end to segregation. It was segregation's failure to maintain separate but <u>equal</u> facilities. We now have to look at the current situation and ask ourselves if it is really working. Clearly the facilities are still not equal. Furthermore, people of the same race tend to live together. So unless you force the issue, it is nearly impossible to have a racially balanced school. Such attempts are often realized through busing programs. It's seemingly always the Black kids that are forced to wake up extra early to go to a school across town. Not only are their parents inconvenienced, the students are typically isolated by white students and ignored by white teachers. Who does this even benefit? If I were a white parent, I would question how adding Black students to an already successful program would benefit my child. Even in racially balanced schools, Black students are lagging behind in several academic categories. So where is the benefit in integration?

Should race be a factor when it comes to education? Should we make academic adjustments due to race? Race matters in every other aspect of life from sports, to Corporate America, to entertainment. So why then should education be any different? Did you ever stop to think about the way African-American History is taught in school? In America, the public schools teach a Eurocentric history. This means that history is told from the perspective of white America. That's why your history seems to begin with slavery, because that's when we became useful to America. Perhaps even more critical than History are the comparably low expectations white teachers have for Black students. Low expectation is the reason high school counselors suggest trade schools for Black students, and four-year universities for white students. Even in school systems where the majority of the students are Black, the majority of the teachers are typically white. The school systems seem less concerned with a culturally diverse staff than they do with a culturally diverse student body.

A Black teacher's ability to identify with a Black student would logically make a Black teacher more ideal for several reasons. Language is critical to education, and although I don't believe in Ebonics, it's helpful if a teacher can comprehend commonly used slang. This becomes particularly advantageous when teaching proper writing skills.

As mentioned earlier, students often have distracting personal issues. Although both white and Black students have personal issues, the types of issues are usually particular to certain races. A Black teacher is more likely to empathize with Black student as they are more likely able to relate to the problem. Simple cultural differences such as the way we punish our children can become a problem for white teachers instructing Black students. What we consider to be a standard whipping, or should I say *woopin'*, might be considered child abuse in white America.

One of the most critical aspects of a child's academic success is his or her level of confidence. Confidence is gained through a combination of encouragement, optimism, and proven success. Encouragement is where teachers and parents come into play. A parent encourages a child whether they believe in the child or not because of their love for the child. With a teacher however, love isn't guaranteed. Expectation now becomes the determining factor, and we all know there is the risk of lower expectations from white teachers. Without encouragement, it's difficult for a child to be optimistic. Without optimism, he or she will rarely succeed.

We complain about the conditions of our public schools. But Black America now has the resources to take the matter of education into our own hands. We spend money on designer clothes, entertainment, and other luxury items. Perhaps we should form more Black-owned and operated private institutions. Facilities would no longer be a factor because we would no longer depend on government funding to provide the adequate facilities our children deserve. Maybe it's time for us to stop voting against a school voucher system, and accept that the public schools have failed us. Or maybe you'd prefer to wait for the government to fix a problem that they probably aren't even capable of fixing. America only works because its individual citizens take action to make things the way they want them to be. In the past, we've waited for the government to fix things. How has that turned out for us?

Answer to 23:

It was the great Malcolm X who questioned Black Americans as to how we measured progress. When we won the right to vote, was that truly progress? Was the Emancipation Proclamation truly progress? Should I be ecstatic when my captors release me, when I shouldn't have been a captive in the first place? Should I do flips and cartwheels because you finally recognize me as a human being? In order to avoid losing a well-supported theory in the midst of emotion-driven argument, it is necessary to focus on the real issue at hand.

The fundamental condition of Black Americans has not changed. In order to understand this point of view, it is helpful to examine the Civil Rights Movement. What were we trying to accomplish? What motivated The Movement? Was it as simple as a woman on a bus? Or was it something far more complicated? The Civil Rights Movement was a response to our condition as Black Americans. That condition was one in which we were taxed the same, but not afforded the same use of the services and facilities our dollars funded. The condition was one in which our average income was far lower when compared to white Americans. The condition was one in which white Americans controlled all our resources. The condition was one in which the business world, and thus employment opportunity, was dominated by white Americans. The condition was one in which police brutalized and terrorized Black Americans. The condition was one in which political-power was dominated by white Americans. The condition was one in which a Black man earned less money than a white man with the same job. Now let's compare the conditions of the past to the conditions of the present. We're still taxed the same, but we obviously don't get the same resources. The public school system proves that. Our average income is still lower than that of white Americans. White America still controls all of our major resources. Who do you pay your utilities to? The business world is still dominated by white Americans, and we have a higher unemployment rate than they do. Police brutality still burns like wildfire throughout our communities. White Americans still dominate politics, and Black men still earn less than a white man doing the same job. So you have to ask yourself: "Have things really changed all that much?" The fundamental principle that caused our problems in the first place still remains. The problem isn't that Black and White can't get along. The problem is that one of the colors has all the control. In our efforts to integrate, many of us failed to recognize competition as a determining factor. The United States is about winning. White America understood that Black America played a vital role in the success white America enjoyed. When we made waves, they needed to make an adjustment. But the overall structure never really changed. Fundamentally, everything is like it was. What white America did was implement purposely-visible changes. Laws changed, and we rejoiced. But white Americans still dominated legislature and were able to work around the laws. More importantly, Black Americans remained financially inferior. In some cases however, the doors to employment opportunity opened. Black Americans reaped the benefits, turning us into "super consumers". Opening these doors did take away opportunities for a limited number of white Americans. But Black Americans love to spend money, and spend a far greater percentage of our income than do white Americans. So since white

Americans still owned most of the businesses and resources, giving us more money didn't narrow the financial gap at all. It in fact developed into the constantly moving set of parallel lines Black Americans and white Americans have become. We stopped circulating money within our own communities because now we are "allowed" to shop in *their* stores. The rest is history.

The purpose of this assessment is not to criticize America, but to be honest about our conditions as Black Americans. Although America has not changed much beneath the surface, it still can change. But in order for things to change, we'd need to agree that they haven't, and that's a whole different issue.

Answer to 24:

The perception once was that AIDS is a gay disease. Although this perception has all but faded, AIDS still holds an inaccurate "dirty" image. The fact of the matter is that AIDS has the face of a model, and the body of a Goddess. But why does Black America have more AIDS cases than any other ethnic group?

One factor is the age at which Black Americans are becoming sexually active. The younger someone is, the less likely they are to use protection. A teen is not necessarily comfortable going into a store and buying a condom. Unfortunately, the teen may still be comfortable enough to have sex. Teens are more likely to have sex in a rushed manner, leaving no time for contraception. But most importantly, a teen typically has the "Invincibility Complex". They never think anything tragic will ever happen to them, so they underestimate the importance of protected sex. In terms of teens and sex, the dynamic of the Black American family also plays a role. A Black child is more likely than any other race of child to live in a single-parent household. As such, the chance the child will be alone increases. This means that the opportunities for unprotected sex also increase.

It can take ten years for AIDS to show in an infected person's system, so it is safe to say many individuals contract HIV in their teen years. But the majority of new Black HIV and AIDS cases are young women. Much of this is due to the fact that it is biologically easier for a woman to become infected than it is for a man. But it's time someone got to the real cause, and most studies fail to address the human factors that truly dictate our lives. The bottom line is that people like to have unprotected sex because it feels better. Not only is there a physical benefit, but sex without a condom implies a certain level of trust that both men and women often desire. When in love, most people either assume that their partner is monogamous or have been told that this is the case. The woman assumes that if he's not wearing a condom, he must be being exclusive and he trusts her. The man assumes that if she allows him to go barebacked, she too must be being xclusive, and trusts him as well. Herein lies the danger in assumptions. Sure here may be more scientific explanations as to why Black Americans are more rone to HIV, but the most likely cause is simple carelessness.

Another factor is knowledge of one's health. Most HIV carriers don't know hey are HIV positive, thereby allowing the virus to spread more effectively. Slack Americans are notorious for ignorance concerning our health status. This is artly because a large portion of Black Americans has no healthcare coverage. Furthermore, an HIV test has to be requested. Just because you get a clean bill of health on a regular check-up doesn't necessarily mean you are not HIV.

The general public is unaware of the origin of AIDS. But the consensus on how to keep it from spreading is clear. In terms of HIV and AIDS, the solution nay be more critical than the cause. Know your partner; and then wrap it up anyway. Case closed.

Answer 25:

Black America often fails to distinguish between having money and having wealth. Lots of people have money. To have money simply means that you consistently receive a certain amount of cash, which affords you a certain lifestyle. By our standards, a man with a big house, luxury car, and nice clothes has money. He must have money, because if he didn't, he wouldn't have been able to afford such nice things. As the years go by, Black Americans are gradually getting more money. The issue here is that when we get more money, we get more things.

White America seems to have a better grasp of the concept of what money can do for you. This is because their goal is likely to become wealthy. What's the difference you ask? Wealth is money that you have, but don't really need. Wealth is there whether you go to work or not. Now ask yourself how many Black Americans you know are wealthy.

Black Americans often define financial growth as an increase in revenue. However, financial growth is measured by net profit, not revenue. In other words, it's not about how much you make; it's about how much is left after you've paid your bills. As Black Americans, we define financial success in terms of the expensive items we have. Unfortunately, most of the items are purchased on credit, and most of the items also depreciate. We all know someone with nice things, but if he or she lost their job, would they be able to keep the nice things? If they had true wealth, the answer would be yes. The truth of the matter is that in Black America, and America in general; most people are living paycheck to paycheck. As convincing as luxury homes and cars can be, you can never really tell who has money versus who has wealth. The problem most of us have is our simple desire

to have so many things. By our rationale, if we have the money, we can afford it.
But life is known for throwing curves, and the only remedy is savings. A lack of
savings keeps thousands of Black American kids from going to college. It keeps
thousands more from spending the rest of their natural lives paying back student
loans. It's how cars are repossessed, and why homes are foreclosed. It's why so
many Black businesses fail so quickly, or never get started at all.

Most of the nation's wealthiest people have made the bulk of their money by
investing. The concept is simple. You spend money on something now, and give
it time to grow. Familiarity with the investment world is common in most white
American families, but foreign in ours. We label stocks, bonds, and mutual funds
as complicated. Investment is not a common part of Black American culture; at
least not important as it should be. The problem is that by the time the bills are
paid, most people have nothing left to invest. This is because investing requires
foresight. One needs to design his or her budget to include investment.

Accumulating wealth is critical to the progress of Black America. In order to
achieve this, we must first alter our thinking. Don't be afraid to sacrifice a few of
your luxury items for the sake of true financial stability. We must remember that
it's not about the money; it's about the wealth.

Answer to 26:

I live in Atlanta: home of the Mega-church. Never in Black America had I seen
more large churches than in Atlanta. With thousands of members comes thousands of dollars in tithes and offerings, and the Mega-church minister can afford
more than the typical Old School Caddy. So the issue arises concerning pastors,
ministers, reverends, bishops, and how well they should be compensated. The big
question is, "Should a pastor be rich?"

Many believers say no. When we talk Mega-churches, we're talking about
Christianity, whether it be Baptist, Methodist, Non-denominational, etc. Christ
certainly breathed humility, and it is an understood goal of any Christian to be as
Christ-like as possible. Therefore, it would seem that a minister who lives in a
mansion and drives a Bentley would be contradicting the very beliefs of which he
teaches. Some feel that excess salary money could be put into church programs
that would benefit more than just the pastor's pockets.

Perhaps it's not bad to have expensive things as long as it doesn't distract you
from the things that are truly important. This seems to be the consensus these
days, especially for those ministers regularly preaching the **Buy a Blessing Philosophy**. I visited a large Baptist church a year ago that has an interesting routine
involving offering. Everyone places their offerings in the standard tithes and

fferings envelopes. The congregation is instructed to waive their envelopes in the air, and is then prompted to repeat a chant in which they announce that they hope to receive things like "Bills cancelled and decreased, unplanned checks in the mail," and other such good fortune. The concept is that you cannot expect good things to happen for you if you don't pay your tithes and offerings. This particular church is just one of many churches encouraging such beliefs. Now I'm no theologian, but since when is God for sale? How can you bribe someone who doesn't need your money in the first place? The Bible clearly states that the meek shall inherit the Earth. It also says that it is easier for a camel to pass through the eye of a needle than it is for a rich man to enter the gates of heaven. Why would a pastor want to be rich? Wouldn't that make it harder for him to get to heaven?

What many find hard to swallow is the fact that a church is a business. It survives on the contributions of its members, much like a country club. They often have television and radio shows, and they advertise like a business would. Mega-churches may have a non-profit tax status, but in all honesty, they usually have more revenue than most other Black-owned businesses. In any business, as the profits increase, so does the CEO's compensation. The bigger the company, the more the boss can be paid. Leading a Mega-church is a full-time job, and pastors deserve full-time pay. For those of you readers in supervisory positions at work, here's a question for you. Would you give up some of your salary because your employees felt that you made too much? Should a pastor of a church with 300 members be paid the same as a pastor heading a church of 30,000? More members equates to more work and more responsibility. Isn't growth the whole idea? Any ambitious church wants to spread its message to as many people as possible. More money and resources come along with new members.

The bottom line is that much of this issue is due to misplaced focus. Church members should be focused on God, not the man whose job it is to interpret God's message. It's not up to you to judge the pastor. Your focus should be on your own life and your relationship with God. Once you do that, you won't really care what the pastor is driving.

Answer to 27:

What in the world is "good hair"? Why is straight hair better than kinked hair? Is a European better than an African? For some, the term "good hair" refers only to the manageability and ease of maintenance straight hair possesses. But in some cases, there is a more troubling definition.

It is quite possible that the feelings many of us have concerning hair have to do with our programmed definition of beauty. As young boys and girls, we

watched a T.V. world filled with European images of beauty. Whether you recog
nize it or not, you likely internalized these definitions of beauty during your for
mative years. Television is often used as the ultimate tool of racism. Only recentl
have we even seen darker skinned Black females on screen. It is no wonder tha
we associate glamour with straight hair. This is the power of psychology. For th
most part, the common application of such an ignorant description of our hai
involves little to no thought. Most have never actually stopped to investigat
exactly why they describe straight hair as good. It is no more than a descriptior
they use because they heard it used sometime before. However, words have valu
only because they have meaning. Unfortunately for Black Americans, those whc
expose the racist backgrounds in words are often viewed as radical conspiracy the
orists, and are not taken seriously.

This issue, at its basis, is almost identical to the issue of lighter versus darke.
skin.

We must take the time to examine the beauty we possess, removing our pre
conceived notions of beauty. As Black Americans, we can take pride in the
strength and natural moisture of our hair. For many, this issue boils down tc
whether or not we are truly glad to be who we are.

Answer to 28:

Visit your local public elementary school in February, and you'll find that Amer
ica sums-up Black History with Dr. King. None can question his accomplish
ments. But there is another great man whose accomplishments are regularly
deemed as controversial. Malcolm X is often swept under the preverbal rug. The
reasons at first appear obvious, and those reasons deserve examination. There is
however a deeper purpose, and as such, deeper consequence.

Before Malcolm's pilgrimage to Mecca, and before being betrayed by his men
tor, Malcolm sometimes referred to whites as *devils*. Although this description is
both harsh and offensive, Malcolm certainly justified it as best possible. Who bet
ter personifies Satan than one whose very country was essentially gained by way
of genocide? It is in fact these same individuals who raped Africa, India, and
North America. But it was all done in the name of imperialism, a nice non-abra
sive synonym for greed. Still, people don't usually want to hear the truth about
themselves uncensored, if at all. Although Malcolm ultimately reconsidered his
initial assessment, the damage was already done.

Contrary to misinformed opinion, Malcolm did not promote violence. Mal
colm stood behind our Constitutional right to defend ourselves; a right appar
ently reserved only for white Americans. Such a platform was easily distorted and

displayed as violent. In the openly oppressive society that was The United States of America, Black Americans were expected to receive any violence against us with a humble "I'm just glad to be alive" attitude. With white on Black brutality being a constant for centuries, the Brothers and Sisters of the 60's had a saturated tolerance for such behavior. Malcolm and others like him represented an intelligent negro who was well aware of his rights as a citizen. Malcolm led a movement in which common sense was coupled with accurate legal and historic knowledge.

White America had accepted Malcolm and Martin as the two voices of Black America. They had similar goals, in that they both pushed for Black American advancement. How they planned to get it, and what they considered advancement were two things on which they disagreed. White America turned healthy debate into media division. Dr. King was projected as the "safe" leader. With his non-violent resistance, and familiar religious affiliation, he became white America's choice. Media credits most of Dr. King's success to his patient marches and non-violent demonstrations. But it was Dr. King's intelligent manipulation of America's economy through boycotting that ultimately sparked the most change.

Malcolm X, on the other hand, was a ready-made villain. He made no attempt to embrace an oppressive white culture. Although a logical reaction, it wasn't the philosophy the media wanted to encourage. Malcolm was not interested in integration. He wanted the U.S. to either give us our own independent land here in the states, or give us provisions to return to Africa. But White America didn't want us to leave, and God knows they didn't want us to be independent. Their economy had grown dependent on our consumerism and labor. Thus, a Black American leader promoting separation certainly had no chance of getting White America's seal of approval.

The fact that Malcolm wasn't Christian warranted isolation. America frequently boasts Christian principals, although it more regularly contradicts them. At the time, Islam was the only religion that specifically addressed and focused on the needs of Black Americans. Islam exhalted the Black man, giving him pride and clear senses of duty and purpose. Such ideals were a frightening prospect to The Powers That Be.

Martin was billed as nonviolent, and Malcolm was billed as violent. In the end, both would suffer violent deaths. What's unfortunate about the Malcolm versus Martin issue is that our young Black Americans are only getting one side of the story. This is a story, mind you, in which the goal should not be to pick a side, rather to learn from both men's accomplishments. Don't expect White America to legitimately integrate Malcolm X into the public school curriculum. If they did, he would not likely be shown in a very positive light. The solution to this issue is no different than any concerning our children's knowledge of true American History, and Black America's more than substantial involvement in its formation. We as Black adults are responsible for first educating ourselves about our real history, and then passing it on to the youth. Otherwise your children will have to depend on White America's remix of American History.

Answer to 29:

Let me first make it perfectly clear that I love hip-hop. In fact, 90% of what I listen to is in some way inappropriate for children. But speaking as a parent, it's becoming more difficult to listen to the radio with kids in the car. So many of the songs are inappropriate for children, if not adults. In case you haven't noticed, "ass" and "bitch" aren't necessarily curse words anymore. "Damn" is on the same level as "darn", and "hell" is just common. Sex is no longer a subject masked with metaphor and innuendo. Now it's just blunt, bold, and in your face. In the past, radio stations would at least wait until after dark before they pulled out the "grown folks" stuff. But now they play it in the middle of the day. What has the radio come to that they'll play such language and content?

The answer is simple. Sex sells. Vulgarity sells. Hardcore sells. A radio station makes a living on advertising. Advertisers will only advertise if people are listening. People listen to what's hot. What's hot these days is often too hot for kids. Unfortunately, they hear it anyway.

It's easy for us on the outside of the music industry to call on artists to take a stand and make songs that everyone could hear. But when your job is to make a hit record, why try to reinvent the wheel? There can only be so many Will Smiths (who incidentally, made his real money in film, not music). Besides, would we as adults be willing to sacrifice our adult content? Some argue that adult content in music is okay as long as you don't play it on the radio. But most people buy an artist's CD because of one or more of the artist's songs they heard on the radio. Even the edited radio versions of explicit songs don't hide much. Anyone can figure out the real lyrics, even kids.

The bottom line is that parents have to be parents. If you don't like what a radio station plays, then turn it off. It's not rocket science. But if you prefer more of an "I'm going to make everyone else adjust to me" approach, you could always contact the station and complain. You could even go so far as to encourage others not to tune in until the station plays more appropriate music. Good luck with that one. But the key to this issue is remembering that as parents, we are still in control.

Answer to 30:

It's almost like an endangered species living in a shrinking environment with limited resources. One would expect the species to be aggressive, and even hostile. But we're not talking about animals. We're referring to Black women. Now Sisters, please don't take offense, because you know we love you. It's just that Brothers want to know why Sisters can't seem to get along. Now many of you Sisters won't admit this is a problem. So I'd like you to take the following quiz and see how you score.

1. When another sister enters the room, do you immediately look her up and down in order to "size-up" your competition?

2. Do you find yourself being critical of celebrity Sisters in ways such as ridiculing their hair or clothes?

3. Do you often find yourself being critical of sisters you don't even know?

4. Do you find it easier to get along with Black male co-workers than Black female co-workers?

5. Do you get along better with Brothers than Sisters?

If you answered "yes" to 3 or more of the previous questions, you just might be a Sister Hater. Although this quiz is all in the name of fun, the implications of a poor relationship between Black women is no laughing matter. Even less funny is the reason behind it.

In the opening, a comparison was drawn between sisters and endangered animals. The situations may be more similar than you think. In Black America however, the Black male is the endangered species. Now regardless of how endangered you feel the Black male is, the perception is that a good Black man is hard to find. In many cases, perception has evolved into reality. If this weren't true, Sisters probably wouldn't be as opposed to Brothers dating outside of their race. But does this warrant negativity and or hostility? Maybe it shouldn't, but it typically does. Watch any pro hockey game and you'll find that tempers often flare for the sake of competition. It isn't that Sisters don't like each other; it's just that they are often after the same thing. Unfortunately, there isn't exactly a surplus on good, available Brothers.

The remedy for Sister to Sister relations does not lie solely on the shoulders of the Sisters, although they do carry the bigger burden. The situation will gradually

improve as the Black American male improves as a whole. Of course, this solution operates under the assumption that the Black male needs improvement. As
always, there's the chance that this is yet another example of a misdiagnosis of the
Black American male. You be the judge. But as for right now, whether it is misconception or truth is inconsequential. Perception is often stronger than reality
and this is the perception of which we are dealing. In the meantime, a Sister first
has to come to terms with why she can't get along with other Black women. If she
finds that competition is the cause, the prescription is confidence. Any brother
will tell you that beyond looking good, and massaging his ego, the best way to get
a man is to be confident. You don't have to put other Sisters down in order to
come out on top. If you demand respect and attention, a man will give it to you.
If he doesn't, would you really want him anyway?

Now Brothers, whether we believe it or not, a Sister's world doesn't necessarily
revolve around us. Until this point, we've focused on competition as the cause for
"Sister Hate". But another, and perhaps more common cause, is simple jealousy.
Women don't only want to look nice for men; they want to look good for themselves. Jealousy is just a part of human nature, and with a sect of population as
beautiful and accomplished as Black women, the bar is set pretty high. This issue
is really one of self-esteem. People who are truly satisfied with themselves rarely
have negative words to say about others. Black women are desirable for reasons
ranging from physical beauty to financial prowess. As such, it is quite understand-
able how a less confident Sister could develop an inferiority complex. You've got
to love who you are, because the worst type of Sister Hate is hating yourself.

Answer to 31:

Before the stereotypical drug and crime-filled American community we know
today, there was a different ghetto. Initially, the ghetto was simply a way to iso-
late Black Americans. Even the Projects was a safe place once upon a time. But
things have changed. Now the ghetto is synonymous with words like poverty and
violence. How did it get this way, and why does it have to be like this?

Anyone can see that crime is the ghetto's greatest downfall. It is true that a
man is responsible for his own actions. But a man's actions are also a response.
The frustrations that lead to violence are typically either the direct or indirect
results of limited opportunity. Simply put in Ebonics terms: "It ain't no jobs!"
The modern ghetto has a concentration of individuals with limited resources,
limited career skills, and limited income. What is not limited however is their will
to survive. For some, the necessity is income, and not necessarily legal income.
Most of the factory jobs that provided Black Americans with opportunities are

ong gone. Without the factory job, the qualifications to be employed become greater. These days, even a four-year degree won't give you an edge. There has always been a correlation between financial status and education. In a capitalist society, the poor are often poorly educated. This is the vicious cycle that is the ghetto.

To complicate matters further, there is another agent. Drugs own the ghetto. With their addictive nature and potential to create quick, substantial, tax-free income, drugs are a seemingly perfect fit for many downtrodden Black Americans. In the narcotics industry, both the consumers and producers yield negative outcomes. A dealer can't sue a client for delinquent payment, or for handling business in an unethical manner, because he himself is breaking the law. Judgement is often handed down by way of bullets. In a criminal world, whom can you trust? Violence is a natural consequence of an illegal lifestyle.

But does the ghetto truly have to be violent? In order for violence in the ghetto to cease, we need more employment opportunities, and no drugs. Both problems are difficult to solve. The fact that the ghetto is filled with low-income families is quite the deterrent for would-be vendors. Even still, opportunity doesn't have to be in the ghetto, just accessible. What has to increase overall is the amount of opportunities for non-professional work. We need more jobs for people who are smart enough to follow directions, be on time, and make a good honest living. Unfortunately, most of those jobs are getting sent overseas or replaced by computers. But the U.S. government doesn't seem interested in protecting its citizens from such occurrences with any real sense of urgency. So as Black Americans, it is our burden to replace those jobs ourselves. The process would likely begin through Black ownership and operation of local businesses such as grocery stores and retail stores. By circulating wealth within our own communities, we could create more Black community businesses. This would create more employment opportunity.

Another approach to solving lack of employment is improvement in education. The premise is that better education will yield more diplomas and degrees, thereby increasing one's chances of securing employment. Improved education also increases the amount of Black entrepreneurs, a result we should more often encourage.

Solving the drug problem is in all honesty, a global issue. But like the triangle trade, the U.S. is a key point in the transaction. Although drugs have taken their toll on the suburbs, the Black American ghetto is the perceived cornerstone of distribution. Those benefiting the most from the sale of illegal narcotics don't live in the ghetto; they employ the ghetto. The ghetto's inhabitants take all the risk, and absorb all the destruction. For every young ghetto drug dealer that falls, two more are waiting to replace him. At some point, the ghetto has to stand up and say "no more". To do that, you probably need to be willing to risk death. However, reluctance and ineffective law enforcement discourages such attitude because citizens don't feel protected.

So it would seem that the ghetto is doomed to be violent. But like any community entity, the ghetto is no greater than the sum of its parts. As such, if the individuals in the ghetto realize that they have a choice, violence in the ghetto could decrease. In many ghettoes violence has in fact decreased over the last decade. Living with limited resources is a struggle; there's no getting around that reality. But pride and humility can co-exist. Many a Black American has risen from the ranks of the impoverished to acquire wealth. They didn't have many employment opportunities, but they had a will to find legal ways to get paid. They had the patience to wait for their education to really start working for them which is unfortunately, something you'll likely have to do. Also, they worked to take care of needs, not wants. Most people in the ghetto can make enough to meet their needs. But needs don't include things like designer bags, jewelry, and luxury cars. Yet and still, there are those ghetto soldiers who do have their priorities in order and are still struggling. If you're struggling, that means you're still surviving. As long as you're surviving, you have a chance to get the life you want.

Answer to 32:

This is a case where the "why" is less important than the result. But the "why" is still worth investigating. Like most things, its roots lie in money. For lack of better terminology, some of our Black athletes and entertainers play the role of high priced whore to the pimp that is the American Media. Although the aforementioned metaphor has negative connotation, athletics and entertainment have empowered many a Black American male. If it weren't for the fruits of commitment, persistence, and expertise, many of our famous Brothers wouldn't be able to positively affect so many. Doing what you love and getting paid for it is the American Dream. Who better represents that than the Black American male athlete or entertainer? The issue however is not representation, but a lack of diversity and balance within that representation.

Despite the slim-to-none odds of making it as a professional athlete or famous entertainer, you can't convince most Black parents that their son isn't the next big star. This only becomes a problem when children and parents view these alternatives as their only real way to riches. Given what you'll find on T.V., who could blame them? The only Black male millionaires on television are either athletes or entertainers. Of course, there are rare exceptions to the rule. But for the most part, a Black man on T.V. is either running, rapping, acting, or singing. Of course running could be for some sport, or very well could be for escaping the law. Either way, it leaves our young Black males with a limited scope.

Is there a conspiracy? Does the media purposely limit its exposure of successful Black businessmen or other professionals? Or is it that an athlete or entertainer is, well, entertaining? That is the whole purpose of television. Even the news has to get ratings. The Black male athlete and or entertainer dominates the tube because he is talented.

The problem is that there is a lack of balance. If we're going to show our kids LeBron James, we also need to show them Willie Gary. It's great that they admire Usher, but can they appreciate the work of Tavis Smiley? When examining some of Black America's successful entertainers or athletes, why not focus on the many business-endeavors these celebrities are regularly involved in? Also, as mentioned earlier in the book, our children need everyday examples of success. Many of our teenage Black American males have become fixated on athletics or entertainment as a career. There's nothing wrong with dreaming, but numbers don't lie. The numbers say that finding success in such a career choice is highly unlikely. Just because something isn't impossible doesn't mean a child should pursue it while ignoring any alternatives. As a former college athlete, I can remember being told to have a back-up plan in case I didn't make it pro. But athletics was always my back-up plan, and education came first. Unfortunately, I cannot say the same for many of my fellow Black athletes. But again, we always saw successful Black athletes. *Cribs* doesn't tour homes of rich professionals, now does it? There's nothing wrong with being a pro athlete or entertainer. But our boys need to know that you don't have to be strong, fast, or have a great voice to be a successful Black man.

Answer to 33:

American propaganda suggests that American principles are based on equality. The concept that all men are created equal has served as a foundation for the many ideals America boasts. To varying degrees, equality is the present and future expectation of Black Americans. But why is this our expectation?

In case you've forgotten, we were introduced to this land as free labor. In case you've forgotten, we weren't written into the constitution. In case you have forgotten, the American legal system considered us property. Now I know someone is reading this right now sighing and thinking "Yeah, I know all that, but that's in the past." But before you go "moving on", please understand that these realities have shaped and continue to shape our condition as Black Americans. Many of us believe in Dr. King's dream with religious conviction, but fail to recognize the time it would actually take for such a dream to become a reality. The surface of American culture would indicate a more unified nation than does actually exist. Has acceptance occurred where it truly counts? Young white adults may listen to rap, but that won't keep them from getting a job. Being Black on the other hand, just might.

Caucasians represent the dominant culture in the U.S., and so they call the shots. It's *survival of the fittest* in its purest form. But even though history clearly teaches us otherwise, many of us expect white America to embrace us as equals. By definition, dominance requires inadequacy. In any society, the dominant culture cultivates a community that caters to the needs of the dominant culture. This happens not only by design, but by circumstance as well. Mathematically speaking, one might expect our wealth to at least be proportionate to the percentage of the population we represent? But it is not, and life rarely follows the rules of math. There are factors such as employment that determine the success of an ethnic group, and the dominant group typically controls these factors. Such is the case in our winner take all America.

Some would argue that white America is committed to hindering Black Americans. Now of course there are those racist individuals who actually do have such goals. But let me put this simply. It's not that white people don't like us, they just don't really care about us. They don't put as much thought into our needs and wants as many of us would like them to. It is primarily the structure of our society that cultivates the discrimination and inequities we face. True, it's a structure they created in the first place. But it is a structure that was created well enough that it doesn't require 'round the clock maintenance. As white America continues to excel, Black America sometimes consequently suffers. Such is the case in a society in which the disparity between two ethnic groups is so great in so many areas. Although our condition as Black Americans is the result of a combination of intentional, unintentional, and self-inflicted acts; white America shares the burden of correcting many of the mistakes it has made. It is the individual discriminatory actions of whites that continue to plague Black America. It's a judge who unjustly imprisons us. It's the manager that won't hire us. It's the officer who uses racial profiling. It's the bank employee that won't approve the loan. It's the landlord that won't rent to us. Racism in America is strengthened and encouraged on a daily basis.

There are some expectations we have of white Americans that we may never see. Remember that you can easily change the laws, but you can't easily change ninds. What is critical is the context in which we expect equality. For example, Black Americans are behind in education. Now this doesn't have to be a permanent predicament, but it will take a considerable amount of time and effort to change. Some inequities, such as real estate ownership and overall wealth, will likely never reach equality. But if our expectation of equality is one based on equal rights, then this is a reasonable goal for America. At the bare minimum, we can expect that our rights as citizens will not be violated. This is easier said than done, as America regularly fails to properly implement this concept. But rather than focus on expectations we have of white America, we would be better served to work on our expectations of Black America.

Answer to 34:

What is our identity as Black Americans? Every ethnic group has a stereotypical identity. Whites are assumed to be smart, but non-athletic, and ultimately successful. Asians are assumed to be intelligent computer geniuses and scientists. Of course, they all practice martial arts too. Hispanics are assumed to be sex-crazed illegal aliens who work better with their hands than their minds. Black Americans are assumed to be lazy with criminal tendencies, but great athletes and entertainers. Intelligence is not a part of our stereotypical description. What happens when members of an ethnic group start to believe the misconceptions concerning their own race?

I can remember that as a child, I often felt compelled to hide my academic ability for fear of ridicule. As I grew older, I found that I wasn't alone in my plight. Black students would always speak of intelligent Black students in a negative light. It went beyond the standard "nerd" or "geek" descriptions. It was a culmination of low expectations for our own kind. This attitude stemmed well into the high school environment, as more Black students chose to identify with sports and fashion rather than academics. One could argue that the white school environment also turns scholars into outcasts. But there is a big difference. I have attended both predominantly white and predominantly Black schools. White students at predominantly white schools expected to get A's or B's. No one would ever be criticized for academic excellence, only hailed and envied. They had this understood concept that getting poor marks was just unacceptable, and **it was reinforced at home**. White students would sometimes appear to be almost suicidal over a bad grade. This is far from the case in my experience at predominantly Black schools.

All this goes back to the perception we have of ourselves, and how critical it truly is. Millions of Black Americans have suffered the effects of Psychological

Slavery. Psychological Slavery is a condition in which a Black American limit one's self due to previously imposed concepts. The effects of our physical slavery here in the United States have far from dissipated. If you tell someone they can' do something long enough, they'll eventually believe it whether it's true or not Black Americans are bombarded with negative verbal descriptions, and negativ visual images concerning our race. All we hear on the radio is how the Brother only need the sisters for sex. We hear how a young Black man is supposed to be a pimp. We hear that the *drug game* is acceptable. We hear how you had better kil anybody that disrespects you. Our little girls hear about how it's okay to give up your body, as long as the guy gives you money and expensive gifts. They get to watch music videos and see how the Black man will only pay attention to them i they dress provocatively. We always see Black faces of suspects and convicted criminals on the news. When we finally do see a positive male image, he's no known for his intelligence. Even the athletes and entertainers are catching cases.

Success starts at home. But it's not enough to punish our kids when they get poor grades. We have to show them the correlation between good grades and monetary gain. White kids get to see this on a regular basis. Maybe you find this difficult because you're a parent that never did too well in school. Who could better teach how hard it is to make it without a good education? Our overall culture has got to start placing more value on education. If not, there inevitably will be no difference between stereotype and reality.

Answer to 35:

Black Americans spend over 20 billion dollars per year on clothes! I have nothing against buying expensive clothing if you can afford to. But there are a couple of things to be noted when discussing Black expenditures. Is what is on our bodies more important than what is in our heads? Our expenditures say "yes". On average, we only spend about 3 billion dollars per year on education. Whether you spend a lot for a pair of shoes is your decision. However, our clothes should not define us, nor should they cause financial peril. In the movie "Shaka Zulu", Shaka offers an interesting metaphor that is appropriate to our clothing issue. A monkey can be trapped by placing a shiny object inside a box that has an opening just large enough for a monkey to place his hand inside. What the monkey fails to realize is that the opening is not large enough for it to remove its hand while holding the object. The monkey, in actuality, will trap itself because it is too entranced by the shiny object to release it and remove its hand. Racists have jokingly compared us to apes for years. Ironically, many of us act like monkeys when it comes to clothes. We are so mesmerized by high-priced fashion that we can't et it go even when it is evident that our compulsion disallows economic advancement. But unlike a monkey, some of us don't even realize that we are trapped.

Issues like this one are all about prioritizing. Prioritizing goes beyond the simple concept of addressing needs before wants. In the case of clothes, it involves understanding why one is obsessed with designer fashion. Most people just want to look nice. But who are you without the clothes? Does your identity depend on the designer garb you sport? A person with healthy self-esteem has no dependent attachment to his or her clothing, and its purpose serves as little more than functional. Like many categories, physical appearance is no more or less important in Black America than it is in White America. But due to under-representation and misrepresentation, our issues are often magnified. What really separates those with nice things is who still has money after all the purchases are made. Plainly put, white Americans are typically left with more money after they've purchased their expensive clothes. Not to mention the intangible and invaluable commodity that is "white privilege".

Answer to 36:

It would seem that the majority of Black America has embraced the idea of integration. Ideally, the overall concept appears sound. But there is a fundamental flaw to the idea of racial integration. For most people, Integration assumes that the individuals will respect each other's differences while viewing and treating each other equally. I have never understood how anyone could have assumed so much.

Integration is a partnership in which entities come together in order to establish a mutually beneficial relationship. In order for such an arrangement to blossom, both entities must desire the merge in the first place. White America never wanted the merge. Did integration make life better for white Americans? Integration involved introducing competition in the workplace. If you were a white man trying to raise your family, would you have looked forward to that? It was understood that a white person had priority over a Black person in any and every situation. Integration would eventually end that. Integration meant sharing and competing for resources that white Americans once dominated completely. Integration would completely alter a lifestyle whites were comfortable with. If you were white, would you be a fan of integration?

Integration has in many ways made us more dependent. They say that necessity is the mother of invention. When we couldn't be a part of their world, we created our own. It was this type of independence that resulted in wealth within Black America. Unlike today, the Black dollar had a chance to circulate before it exited our communities. No one really argued against "separate but equal". Had America held up to its part of the deal, things would be very different now. Integration was more a less a response rather than a choice. As is the case in most presidential elections, we chose the lesser of two evils. I doubt most Black Americans expected the best outcome, they just hoped for it.

Whether or not integration has helped us is somewhat irrelevant if you don' have an alternative. Integration is by no means ideal, but what alternative do we have? We have successfully separated in the past. Black Wallstreet is a prime example. But like so many examples of separated Black prominence, once we did better than whites did, they destroyed it.

The alternative to integration is separation. Separation is a bad word to some Black Americans. The time has come for an evolved separatist concept. Traditionally, the fundamental premise of Black separatism in America involved Black Americans either leaving the country, or separating within it. Returning to Africa is far from desirable for most Black Americans. We have well-established roots here, and have grown accustomed to and fond of the life America affords us. From a social aspect, separation could be considered regression. But people tend to separate naturally, especially since Black Americans now possess more of the resources necessary to live "the good life'. In many areas, there are luxury communities filled only with Black families. Perhaps we should pursue separation in terms of priority. In other words, we should focus on strengthening our own communities. In most cases, a Black American who started off in a Black community leaves his or her community once he or she becomes successful. These actions do not reflect his or her desire to abandon his or her roots. It is usually a matter of his or her desire for what the Black community cannot provide. Black communities are often devoid of the products and services available in white communities. Should Black Americans deny themselves life's luxuries for the sake of separatism? Such an expectation is unrealistic. A more productive goal would be to focus on adding some of these desirable products and services to our communities. Magic Johnson was able to convince Sony that such a concept could be profitable, as evident in the success of his movie theaters. As other Black entrepreneurs begin to invest in our communities, the Black dollar will circulate within them. This strengthens our communities by adding jobs, increasing property values, and making the areas more lucrative to many of the types of businesses we wish to patronize.

Separation is first achieved mentally. We must accept that despite more generic concerns, Black and white Americans often have different and sometimes conflicting priorities. Being different is really only a problem when we are all competing for the same resources. The problem is that Black Americans are often competing for resources controlled by the competing group. Furthermore, an individual is better equipped for, and more likely to succeed in a society designed by his or her kind. We now have the ability to strengthen, shape, and cultivate growth in our own communities. We could create schools designed to meet the needs of Black students. We could provide grocery stores that carried items essential to the dietary needs and wants of our culture. We could have our own banks so that more of us could actually get a fair loan. We could have our own hospitals and other such medical facilities where doctors would be familiar with Black healthcare issues and concerns. We could have all of these things right in our own communities. But we first have to be willing to separate.

Answer to 37:

Why do we feel it is okay to be late? We have even coined the affectionate term, "C.P. Time". Tardiness itself may be little more than a nuisance for some, but it leads to more damaging behavior. Being late sometimes just boils down to a lack of concern for others. But the bottom line is that there's no excuse for it. Of course there will be situations that would cause anyone to be late. But being late regularly is just ridiculous. Even more ridiculous is the fact that we seem to expect and accept it. Such behavior is indicative of what we accuse white America of saying we are, yet we tend to do a great job of supplying supporting evidence. We take for granted the little things like this. But it's these little things that build to contribute to and form bigger problems. Black Americans and our perceived inability to be on time translates into our inability to compete in professional arenas. Would you deliver a critical overnight package with a Black-owned company? Would you want your EMS service to be Black? If you flew on a Black-owned airline, would you be confident that your flight would take-off on time? Suddenly it doesn't seem so cute and trivial, does it?

Answer to 38:

When it comes to unemployment, a Black man has four main enemies: technology, foreign countries, education, and himself. Unemployment is soaring in America, and our Brothers and Sisters are feeling it the most.

Technology is the result of mankind's need to conquer inconvenience. It is his quests for knowledge and a better life that drive his desire to become technologically advanced. But for every door that technology opens, it closes ten. Black Americans dominate the low to middle-level job segment, even though the Hispanic population is close to replacing us in that role. Computers now threaten once secure jobs, like those in plants and factories. In most cases, a computer is as or more efficient and productive than a human being. Plus, companies save money on the benefits plans, workman's compensation, and lunch hours computers do not need. A computer won't call in sick, get pregnant, sue an employer, or hinder morale. Computers pose threats to Black Americans in yet another way. Technology makes the world smaller. People can now work with a company without physically being there. This brings us to the next enemy.

Have you ever called customer service for what you thought was an American company, and ended up talking to someone in India? This sort of thing is happening more often. Indonesia has all but taken over the customer service realm, as well as other occupations. Why is this? It's because in many cases, someone overseas can do just as good a job as someone in the U.S., but at a fraction of the cost. Apparently, supporting the American worker isn't as important as supporting the bottom line. In big business's defense, it's hard to be competitive these days without taking advantage of overseas employment. But the effect it has on Black America is devastating.

There is a clear correlation between education and income. Typically, the more education one has, the more income one is likely to earn. For Black America this reality is troublesome, as we rank last in almost every category of education. This disparity is most clearly seen when comparing our academic resume to that of White Americans. If our young Black Americans are receiving an inferior education, we are sending them into a viciously competitive career-market ill prepared. The competition for jobs begins well before college or even high school graduation. It begins in elementary school when students are first being taught basic skills. It is in a child's early years that he or she develops the ability to learn new information and apply it in such a way that it yields positive returns. Isn't that what making money requires?

There are obviously some very real challenges concerning Black American employment. But there are still those individuals who only have themselves to blame. For many, it is a simple matter of poor work ethic. But the real problem is often lifestyle. In most big cities there are jobs available. The problem is that most of them are not high paying; at least not the ones you can get without a secondary degree. Immigrants will take these lower paying jobs and work them until they can do better. But this isn't usually the case with Black Americans. Why is that? The difference is in the lifestyle. As Black Americans, we tend to desire and attempt to maintain a certain standard of living. We want to look a certain way. We need to eat a certain way. We need to drive certain cars. The average Black American has developed an expectation of a lifestyle that cannot be sustained by a minimum wage job. If you can't make enough money to pay all your bills by working, you might as well just get unemployment checks. This rationale may be ignorant, but it is common, and fairly logical.

Although some unemployed Black Americans are jobless by choice, this number pales in comparison to the number of unemployed legitimately trying to find work. So what is one to do? Low income is better than no income. So if you can find one, work a minimum wage job, even if it won't pay all your bills. Make as much as you can, and pay the important ones. Your credit will likely suffer, but you'll survive to fix that later. Try a job at a fast food restaurant. The turnover will be high, and there will likely be plenty of locations. This means more opportunity to advance. Many individuals with corporate options choose retail and similar arenas because they offer more opportunities to advance. The hiring process is typically faster and less complex than the corporate structure, and time is everything when you're unemployed.

In the long run, education is the key to employment. It allows you to become more competitive, and it gives you the skills to become self-employed if you so choose. Self-employment is a great remedy to the threat of unemployment, because no one can lay you off. But not everyone has the skill, work ethic, or desire to be an entrepreneur, so this may not be a realistic option for you.

In the end, sometimes there is nothing you can do about unemployment. This is an American reality. What you can do however is be prepared in case it happens. You've got to keep bills low. If you can buy things with cash, do that. If not, then maybe you shouldn't buy it. Now of course there are exceptions like a home, a car, or some emergency. But even with homes and cars, there is the opportunity to purchase within your means. You never know when you might become unemployed, so plan as if you know you will be, just to be safe.

Answer to 39:

Our soldiers deserve the utmost respect and gratitude for risking life and limb for all of us. But as in any time of military conflict, Black Americans ask themselves where they stand in the war.

One of the issues adding complexity to warfare in America is the fact that our country is not truly united. Although we'd like to believe we're all in this together, the truth is that the U.S. is somewhat of a conglomerate of different ethnic groups with independent agendas. We are all geographically bound together, and thus we all feel the effects of war. The effects however are not identically allocated. At the root of war itself is the soldier. The question is whether or not an American soldier should be Black.

Our lives as Black Americans have been based on response. We're alway
recipients, adapting in order to survive. Our involvement in the U.S. military i
no exception. Like most career options, most are in it for the compensation, no
the passion. It would seem that this is common as it pertains to Black America
soldiers. There's a reason military recruiting is so prominent in the ghetto. Th
military provides a solid alternative to the unemployment and crime many youn
Americans face. It offers money, education, and a "sense of purpose". Even if th
latter doesn't move you, the first two benefits are definitely worth considering
What do you do with no job, little education, and little hope? The military is on
of the few legal options you have. However, there is always the significant chanc
you could be killed. For many Black soldiers, service to the country is no mor
than a hazardous job. Truth is, if it weren't for the regularly challenging economic environment that Black America faces, there would likely be few Black soldiers. What rational Black American would be eager to risk life and limb for a
country that has treated us so poorly for so long?

There are those however who do identify with America, and feel that military
service is their civic duty even before the brainwashing propaganda the military
imposes. One could argue that given our history here as Black Americans, it is
unintelligent to support such a nation with one's life. The Constitution we so
vigorously defend never included us as citizens in the first place. Black Americans
have always fought for rewards less rewarding than those afforded to our Caucasian counterparts. So is this all in the past? By and large, most Black Americans
are not pleased with the way America treats us. Monetary gain aside, one could
argue that the military is no place for the Black American. Reports of racism
within military ranks are quite common, even though The Service is billed as the
one professional arena where racism is not a factor. For one to even expect such
an idealistic reality is ludicrous, especially since the military was segregated in the
first place. Are we to believe that the U.S. Military has somehow managed to successfully evolve its race relations where the rest of America has failed?

Though racism might be a minor deterrent, it isn't the primary reason Black
Americans don't belong in the military. We have to be honest about who we are.
Most of us are descendants of slaves. Although we are generations removed, the
transition has been far from smooth. From a fundamental aspect, how logical is it
to aid one's oppressor? The problem with this ideology however is that Black
Americans are in such a position where we cannot help but to aid our oppressors.
Just about everything we do aids white Americans. Everything we buy, every bit
of technological progress we create, and every skill we offer, contributes to America's prosperity as a whole. The dominant culture never really loses, and we have

ong since established the identity of the dominant culture. This being said, we have to now focus on how Black America can benefit. It is no secret that oil is at the heart of our current conflict with the Middle East. If conquest there will nsure a more prosperous American lifestyle, than perhaps it could be seen as jus-ifiable for Black Americans to participate. I however am inclined to disagree.

Why send our Black youth off to die when they could be here living and help-ng our communities to grow? With the limited amounts of accurate and relevant nformation the American public is truly privy to, it is often difficult to know vho really benefits from any war. As such, we must examine the past to see just ow warfare has benefited Black America. The last time warfare had any particu-ar positive effect for us was the Civil War, and that was simply an issue of crip-ling The South by removing their free labor. The most common effects consist of Black soldiers returning home with chemical dependencies, permanent "uni-dentifiable" illnesses, physical and mental impairments, and no jobs. Black Amer-ca's war is not being fought overseas; rather it is being fought right here at home.

Black Americans may share ethnicity, but we have very different opinions of our condition. In terms of service to the country, where we think we fit becomes critical. Black Americans have always looked ahead. Typically, it's all we can do. Although America is far from perfect, it would seem we're going to be here. As such, it is not necessarily illogical to want to defend America. However, our mod-ern era of televised warfare brings to light new concerns as to the true motivation for war. This leads citizens to see themselves as individuals rather than a cohesive unit. To some, it appears that the president has selfish motivations. Such conclu-sions encourage citizens and particularly soldiers to question whether or not they should be at war. Soldiers begin to ask themselves questions like: "What will be left for me when I get back to The States?" The multitudes of struggling Vietnam Vets could easily answer such questions; although our president probably doesn't want to hear their answers. Overall, Black America does not benefit from military service any more than any other ethnic group. But like any other contribution we make to America, military service is somewhat justifiable if it is something Black Americans could use as leverage in an attempt to improve one's individual condi-tion. From a fundamental standpoint, maybe it isn't bad to have your country's back. But you have to ask yourself: "Does my country really have my back?"

Answer to 40:

When it comes to religion, individuals defend their beliefs with a passion like no other. But historically, there is but one truth. So let us examine this question from that respect.

Documentation validates history. So for the sake of this inquiry, we shall begin by making reference to a common document. The Bible is a suitable reference point, particularly for most Black Americans. Though their reasons for reading it may be different; Christian, Jewish, and Islamic people consider at least some parts to be accurate. Christianity, Judaism, and Islam dominate American culture, and two of the three are top contenders for the title of The Black Religion. The origins of all three are clearly addressed, and intertwined. Of the three the Bible indicates Judaism as the first. Judaism obviously pre-dates Christianity because Jesus himself was born a Jew. Islam stems from Abraham. The Bible explains that Abraham prayed for a son, but grew impatient. He then conceived a child by his wife's handmaid. Ishmael was born. But later, God blesses Abraham with Isaac, the son he was promised in the first place. Isaac was born of Abraham's wife Sarah, so Abraham banished Ishmael and his mother Hagar into the desert. God hears Hagar's sorrowful prayers, and consoles her explaining that Ishmael will father a great nation. Ishmael goes on to be responsible for the birth of the Nation of Islam. These details bring to light the theory that Allah, Yahweh, and God are all the same entity.

In America, most Black Americans are either Baptist Christian, or Non-denominational Christian. This reality seems odd, if not illogical, as Christianity was a key controlling factor in the institution of American slavery. Whites manipulated verses such as "slaves, obey your masters", and even today white supremacists (and sadly, Black ministers) continue to contort the Bible to fit their needs. For most slaves, Christianity represented the destruction of all they'd ever believed. We were Christians by consequence, and not by choice. Certainly, the majority of our ancestors did not practice Christianity, although Christianity spread sparsely into Northern Africa before slavery began in America. It is therefore possible, but unlikely, that some of our ancestral captives were in fact Christian. Still, Christianity provided hope for the slaves. Many believe that it was the Christian God who delivered us from slavery. This belief, along with undeniably instrumental influence in the Civil Rights Movement, has all but crowned Christianity as the Black American Religion.

For some however, Islam became recognized as the Black Religion with the rise of Malcolm X. Though its association with the Black race may have been as much strategy as truth, Islam has a much larger African following than does Christianity. In the 1960's, The Nation of Islam was the only religion to specifically focus on the challenges faced by Black Americans. Not only did it address the issues, it offered practical, and relatively immediate solutions. But if the chronology of religious origin is of any importance, The Nation of Islam may not satisfy would-be believers. Of late, The Nation of Islam's U.S. presence carries a different face, at least to those whose knowledge of its existence is limited to America. The new face of Islam is Middle-Eastern. Unfortunately, both an Arab face and The Nation of Islam are associated with terrorism. As more and more Americans become patriotic, they are becoming less interested in investigating the truth about Islam. With anti-terrorist rhetoric looming, it's easy to hate Islam in ignorance.

For the most part, Black Americans find discomfort in the concept of polytheism. Polytheism is the belief in more than one god. Yet Ancient Egyptians, members of what is arguably the most advanced civilization ever to exist, were polytheistic during most of Egypt's mighty reign. There are a small but growing number of Black Americans with polytheistic beliefs. Religions such as Ifa and Kemetics are more common with Black Americans of island descent, and are often confused with voodoo and other such practices. But I would wager that if properly explained, most open-minded individuals would have to admit that concepts such as polytheism, reincarnation, and ancestral worship are more rational than many might assume. Ancestral worship has always been a staple in African tradition. But to "African-Americans", what our ancestors have always done is somehow so easily tossed aside even without the help of our regularly accused white Americans. When it comes to religion, logic is all but irrelevant; and like most things in America, it's the packaging that really counts. Ifa and Kemetics have too many American Negro barriers to conquer. For these such faiths, religion is no different than music. Sometimes an album can be really great; but that doesn't mean it sells well.

Which religion you consider to be the Black religion depends on how you define Black. I define Black as the American of African descent, introduced primarily by way of slavery. Too disconnected from our homeland and not truly accepted here, we really have no home. Black Americans are essentially floaters, holding on to a combination of African and American heritage. Because of slavery, few of us can trace our ancestry beyond North American shores. If you aren't certain where you came from, you can't be certain how your ancestors worshipped. In terms of our history in America, Christianity is the consensus religion. But we should also keep in mind that truth is not dependent upon how many people believe in it. Religion was, is, and always should be a personal decision.

Answer to 41:

White people drink too. So why aren't their communities filled with liquor stores? Any business owner will tell you that location is critical to success, so an establishment needs to be convenient to its customers. But are liquor stores in our communities because we love alcohol, or do we love alcohol because liquor stores are in our communities?

The reality is that liquor stores are most commonly found in low-income areas. This holds true even in non-Black neighborhoods. The correlation between society and alcohol is based primarily on economics, not race. But societal structure is not a random occurrence; rather it is the result of specific consistencies. As such, the negative effects of alcohol can be skewed towards a particular race. Simply put, by percentage there are more poor Black Americans than poor white Americans. Therefore, any problems related to low-income communities have larger relative impacts for Black Americans.

From a liquor-store owner's perspective, there are zoning issues to tackle when searching for a location. Local government determines where such stores can and cannot be. In addition to fostering a safe environment, local governments want to encourage revenue flow. The more a business makes, the more tax dollars the business shells out. As most would assume, zoning laws are rarely an issue in the ghetto. More important than tax dollars is creating in environment in which people want to live, visit, and spend money.

Zoning aside, the whole point is to sell as much alcohol as possible. Package stores in the hood rarely fail. If one does fail, it's probably because the liquor store down the street is cheaper. Black Americans are great alcohol consumers. It's no mystery, since our culture constantly spurts references to libation in our music and television. Rappers regularly make songs about drinks, drinking, and getting drunk! The decision to make alcohol readily available to Black Americans is a no-brainer.

Psychology suggests that drinking often goes beyond the need to have a good time. Alcohol is often used as therapy of sorts, or more accurately, a temporary solution that will eventually cause more problems than it solves. Who is more likely to drink than someone who has a lot of problems they'd like to forget, if only momentarily? However, Black Americans do not have an affinity for alcoholism.

Bottom line is liquor stores aren't in suburban white neighborhoods because they ruin communities. Liquor stores lower property values. There is an established correlation between liquor stores and crime. What more do Black Amerians need to know before we decide to disallow liquor stores in our communities? Business is business. If we don't buy, liquor-store owners will go elsewhere. Preserve your community. If you don't, who will?

Answer to 42:

It is unsettling to say the least, that much of what police do is based on profiling. Profiling is the practice of creating a profile, or common description of a criminal. Police claim this method allows them to prevent crimes by recognizing the potential for deviance, and stopping crimes before they happen. According to police, a Black male is the most likely description of a criminal. It is no wonder that "the law" regularly mistreats Black men.

Is their any validity to the claim that most criminals are Black men? In actuality, a criminal is most likely to be a white male. This is largely due to the fact that there are more white males in America than any other type of male. But a Black male is more likely to be incarcerated than a white male is. Nearly half of all prisoners is Black. Yet Black Americans as a whole make up less than 13% of the population. Such data leaves us with two possibilities. Either Black men are innately deviant, or Black men are targets.

The idea that Black men are somehow mentally predisposed to commit criminal acts is ludicrous. There is however an undeniable connection between poverty and crime. In most cases, crimes are committed due to the frustration and desperation poverty causes. All humans have basic needs. The question is whether or not one can find a way to meet these needs legally. Black America has a larger percentage of poor people than does white America, so it is conceivable that this may result in a high crime rate for Black Americans. But there is a combination of perception and reality that defines our existence. We don't exactly shy away from the criminal persona. In fact, our youth embraces it, as heard in the themes of much of our popular music. In time, such a mindset has evolved into real life. Criminal motivations are no longer limited to poverty. Criminal motivations now include such inspirations as boredom, confused identity, and misplaced ambition.

The police, in general, have gained a reputation for abusing their power, particularly in their dealings with Black Americans. But since a police department is no greater than the individuals that combine to form it, perhaps it is unfair to categorize entire police departments as racist. But the identity of any department is molded, encouraged, and ultimately controlled by its leadership. When it comes to racist police behavior, the leaders of criminal justice aren't sending the right signals with their slap on the wrist punishments. In fact, one could argue that the California legal system is responsible for the riots following the Rodney

King verdict. As a Black male, I can say that if given a choice between a confrontation with a thug and a confrontation with a policeman, I'd likely choose the thug. At least if the thug attacks me, I can defend myself without necessarily being killed or doing life in prison.

It is critical that we know exactly what law enforcement is designed to do. The words *law* and *enforcement* seem to be self explanatory. However, there remain the question of whether or not police in fact create criminals. Take your average police sting operation for example. A sting is when officers do things like pose as prostitutes or leave an unlocked car in a poor neighborhood. The police entice individuals to commit crimes, and then pat themselves on the backs for arresting them. Your local police department would argue that such operations are quite beneficial, even critical if you will. But you have to wonder just who determines where stings are done? Why are they never done in white suburban areas? Middle and upper-class white kids do drugs just like any other kids, so why don't police pose as drug dealers and try to sell to them? The answers to these questions are more than obvious to most Black Americans. In sting operations, some detainees weren't criminals until posed with the situation the local police department manufactured. The reality however is that as long as Five-O thinks they work, sting operations won't stop. But aren't there enough crimes being committed without the help of the police to keep them busy? Even still, it is likely that officers will busy themselves by harassing Black communities.

One possible solution to our problems with police could be a simple matter of placing Black officers in Black neighborhoods. Theoretically, a Black officer will be more familiar with our culture. A Black cop should understand that hip-hop fashion doesn't equate to deviance, or that braiding your hair doesn't make you a criminal. Most importantly, citizens are more likely to trust an officer that looks like them. The best officer is one with ties to the community in which he serves. Such an officer is more likely to be concerned with the well being of that community. Police departments should offer incentives for officers to stay in the community in which they police. These incentives could include lower-cost housing, salary increases, or bonuses.

Most parents have "the sex talk" with their preteen sons. In addition to "the sex talk", Black American boys need to have "the cop talk". It's an unfortunate reality that when you're Black, the police may not be your friend. They'll likely search you without just cause, ask you to "move along" for no reason, you'll get a ton of undeserved traffic stops, and you may even get beaten or killed. Even when cops use excessive force, our best bet is to fight back in court. Not that we'll win, out at least we'll be alive. It's a sad philosophy isn't it? But how far from the truth is it?

People may criticize the original Black Panther Party, but they dramatically reduced the rate of police brutality in Oakland during their time. They educated citizens about their rights, and used the Constitution as their shield. They armed the citizens, which is our Constitutional right, and trained them in the art of self-defense. They brought the community together and represented each other as a group. If you brutalized one Panther, you had all of them to deal with. They had party members on patrol, not only to make sure police did not abuse their power, but to help protect their own communities. Maybe it's time we learn from the Black Panthers' example and implement some or all of these practices. Like all our problems as Black Americans, they won't ever be solved if we wait for the solution to come from the outside.

Answer to 43:

I am a slave
—a poem written by Byron F. Wilson

Sold on the auction blocks at Charleston; I am a slave.

I once ran free through the vast deserts of Egypt,

Leapt the Mighty Victoria Falls,

Navigated the treacherous Congo,

Conquered the Sudanese sun.

But now, at the hands of my sister, I am a slave.

Vengeance captained my ship of passage, while ignorance guided it to port.

In anger, my sister sought profit from my sale.

Blade to the siphon of white-skinned wrath;

She encouraged the rape of my daughter.

She smirked as Satan determined my soul,

Delighted while another devalued it.

She points out the spots on my back to be whipped, and enables the white men to discard my name.

I am strong, yet I must appear weak for fear of merciless judgement.

I am prideful, yet I must hang my head in honor of those I do not
respect.

I must carefully address my oppressor, or I may lose my very life.

Hand delivered by my own sister, I stood unchained, but bonded on
the auction block.

And as the Pale Moon lowered its final decision it yelled, "Sold…to
the lowest bidder!"

I was sentenced to slavery for a length no less than the life of a child.

When my sale became final, my sister was also enslaved, only she
doesn't know it.

The hopes of my family all but destroyed, and altered forevermore.

Now I am at the mercy our new Masters.

How many more will be sold by their own?

This is a piece I wrote in response to the brief, one-sided custody trial for my
daughter. I completely accept my responsibility in the endeavor, as it takes two to
conceive a child. Her mother and I have since established a positive relationship
and she in no way attempts to keep me from my daughter. But what about the
Baby Daddies that aren't as lucky as I am? The fact is that the legal system affords
fathers little power when it comes to children.

Whether a child's custody is in question as the result of unwed parents or
divorced parents, the father rarely sees equality. Courts look to establish a primary parent, the parent the child lives with the majority of the time. In order for
a man to get primary custody over a woman, the woman would have to be a drug
addict, alcoholic, homeless, or abusive. Even then it's hard for the father to win
custody, particularly in the traditionally conservative South. But why is this?

Much of the cause is simply a matter of the courts holding on to the traditional mother and father roles. The father brings home the bacon, and the
mother takes care of the kids. But much of the system is the way it is because of
the typical male response. Particularly in the case of Black American men, fathers
don't exactly have the best track record. Sisters have had the unfortunate tasks of
getting fathers to acknowledge paternity, pay child support, and spend time with
their kids. So the courts stepped in to address all three issues. The problem is that
the inflexibility of the legal system poses a relatively insurmountable obstacle for
the father that is trying to do what he's supposed to. Not only does the legal system make it hard on the father; it also empowers the mother. As much as we'd all
like to believe in the legal system, the fact is that it doesn't always look at individ-

uals as, well, individuals. The all-stars get lumped right in with the deadbeats, and some judges couldn't care less about establishing the difference.

It is the issue of time that seems to hit good fathers the hardest. The courts have devised a standard visitation schedule in which the father gets every other weekend and alternating holidays. Usually, the father ends up with four days per month, a little more than one seventh of most months. The schedule is hardly balanced, but it isn't written in stone. The schedule can be altered, although it rarely is. If it is altered, it is usually by way of mediation. But in mediation, both parties have to agree to the schedule. This puts the power in the hands of the mother since she is all but guaranteed the role of primary parent if a judge makes the decision. Furthermore, unless it is court-ordered, both parents have to agree to meet for mediation in the first place. At the point where the mother refuses, the father is screwed. All of this becomes irrelevant if the mother is amicable and is able to see that a father deserves more time than the standard court visitation schedule allots him. But this is not always the case, particularly in the case of unwed parents. Unfortunately, the father has little protection at this point. Even when the father is granted joint legal custody, as I was, the mother has the final call on all major decisions. Such decisions include school, church, doctors, and any extracurricular activities.

The standard visitation schedule is dangerous in such cases where the mother is, shall we say, not quite fond of the father. A primary parent can easily paint a negative picture of the other parent, and the limited time the child spends with that parent reinforces it. By the time Junior is old enough to understand why he only sees his father every other weekend, a huge amount of damage may already have been done.

The courts have made clear their priority. If you don't have a large sum of money for attorney's fees, you probably won't end up with a lot of time with your child. Even with a great attorney, you'll likely be disappointed if you're looking for more time than the standard visitation schedule. In an ideal world, the legal system would look at each father on an individual basis rather than responding to what has unfortunately become many a Black father's position. But a Black American's world is far from ideal. In the end, all you can do is be the best father you can be. In situations of custody, a man is often at the woman's mercy. Certainly the burden lies with mothers to ensure that personal feelings do not interfere with the relationship between a father and his child. But men cannot assume all women will be able to do this. Black American men cannot allow themselves to be discouraged by scorned women who may not always be able to act in the best interest of the child. We cannot give up on being fathers, no matter how difficult it becomes. Such an effort requires taking advantage of every opportunity to spend time, teach values, and give support. Otherwise, we contribute to the removal of the Black American father, an act that can only lead to the deterioration of Black America.

Answer to 44:

First of all, we must accept that people are simply different. As a result, they will sometimes not get along. This reality is no different for Blacks than it is for whites. It is however magnified in Black America because of our lower relative population, and our consistently unequal socioeconomic condition. Undeniably, one's behavior is influenced by one's mental-emotional state. Think of the behavior of someone in love, versus someone who is depressed. A person in love is more likely to smile for no apparent reason, open doors for strangers, or ignore potentially hostile encounters. Black citizens rarely share the love affair with America that white citizens do. Even when we do, it is often unrequited. The "Black Caste" seems to promote inner-racial competition, as does any condition in which a particular sect of individuals is limited to certain opportunities. America presents a face filled with boundless possibilities for all people; but the problem is that the face is colorless. For every white man a Black man beats out for a position, he has beaten 50 Black men; hence the tension that is Black America.

Sociology aside, there is an even more specific origin of the general discontent we seem to have with our own kind. It's ironic that it still all comes down to field niggas and house niggas. During slavery, we were easily separated by our "appointed positions", if you will. Some of us, typically the darker of us, worked in the fields; while others, the lighter of us, worked in the plantation house. Time changes, but the game remains the same. In modern society, the field nigga has evolved into what we would call the average, *blue collar* worker. He likely works with his hands, and gets paid hourly rather than salary. He has skills that can earn a moderate income; even more than moderate if he can manage to get overtime pay. But the field nigga feels the restrictions of having no real entry into the professional world. He identifies with struggle and work ethic of a physical nature. The field nigga is sometimes mistaken for one who lacks intelligence, yet this is often far from the truth. Very little of the field nigga's income is not designated to bill paying, but he will treat himself. As such, he is surprisingly quite the consumer. The nation depends heavily on the field nigga, and it is literally the field nigga who built America. Yet for all his efforts, he is rewarded with being the Black American most regularly discriminated against. What's worse is the field nigga's world seems to be disappearing, as large corporations shift employment outside of the United States in favor of Asia. But for many a field nigga, it is simply a matter of reinventing himself. This however is easier said than done, and so we have an America filled with frustrated field niggas.

Now the modern house nigga is the professional Black American. Wearing his *white collar*, he climbs his way through the ranks of corporate America, and is often mistakenly labeled a sell-out by the field nigga. As in the days of slavery, the "thriving" house nigga is, more often than not, a female. The house nigga takes pride in the doors his education has opened; that is unless his well-to-do family and friends opened those doors. The house nigga is not lacking in work ethic, and he likely works long hours in the office to compensate for the color of his skin of which he so adamantly denies is a factor. He typically has more money to spend than does the field nigga, and he guarantees the life of the phrase, "keeping up with the Jones'". Although he too feels discrimination, it is not often as bold as the discrimination the field nigga receives. Therefore, the house nigga is prone to exist in a proverbial limbo; trapped between believing Black American inequity is the result of white discrimination, and recognizing that inequity is sometimes the fruit of our own lack of effort. By comparison, the house nigga typically has more resources than does the field nigga. As such, socioeconomic change within Black America relies heavily on them. Unfortunately, the house nigga is often relatively comfortable, and comfort has never provoked revolution.

Re-examining slavery, the bottom line is that whether they were house niggas or field niggas, they were all slaves. Despite some differences, America made sure the slaves had constant reminders that they shared a common predicament. One of the issues Black Americans face today is that not all of us realize we share a common predicament. True, we live in a capitalist country. As such, people separate themselves financially. In theory, one who starts off in the lower-class can end up in the upper-class simply by increasing his wealth. But what many Black Americans fail to recognize is that this theory is only sound as it applies to the majority culture. Put into ghetto terms: "It just don't work that way for Black folks." In terms of Black and white, race means two different things. For us, race manifests itself to be discrimination. For them, it's affectionately called, *white privilege*.

To prove that a white American is privileged is a waste of time, as it is quite simple to do so, and has long since been established. The issue here is the apparent inability for Black Americans to work together. In order to investigate said reality, it is first necessary to define "working together". Working together requires that two or more parties join, whether permanently or temporarily, in order to reach some common goal. All parties involved must offer mutually beneficial contributions in order to maintain a healthy relationship. Although it may sound simple enough, both past and present tell us it is not.

Our biggest problem is establishing a common goal. Ironically, the more options we gain, the further apart we become. Consider our slavery here in the U.S. There were very few conflicting issues between Black Americans; we all just wanted to be free. Once we were "free" however, Black America grappled with the issue of what to do with our new found freedom. Some of us thought we should stay and sharecrop. Others thought The North was the answer. Still, others believed westward expansion to be our best alternative. Time advanced, and so did Black American accomplishment. But as we entered the Civil Rights Era exactly how to go about gaining those civil liberties became yet another issue. Some of us wanted to turn the other cheek, while others believed in an "eye for an eye". Some wanted integration, others championed separation. Today, in what some consider to be our most socially advanced era ever, Black America still grapples with the "what" and "how" of socioeconomic change.

People are searching for a new Black Leader, and we rummage through choices spanning from Jackson, Sharpton, and Farrakhan, to West, Smiley, and Mfume. Yet these gentlemen face almost insurmountable odds. One must recognize the complexity of Black America with its many backgrounds, present realities, and future desires. It is nearly impossible to lead a group of a thousand different agendas. That is unless that leadership accepts, appreciates, and properly channels those differences. Here is where the house nigga and field nigga must come together. Now I am well aware that many of you are so offended by my use of the word nigga, that you may be distracted enough to miss an all-important conclusion. So for the time being, I shall refrain from using the word. Semantics aside, those who have and those who have not must first accept their differences. Please understand that there will always be wealthy Black Americans. There will also always be poor Black Americans, as well as all those in between. One's economic condition heavily influences one's outlook, opportunities, and behavior. It's time we upper-income Blacks accept that the less financially fortunate brother isn't necessarily being negative about whether or not he'll get that high-paying job. Maybe in his world, he's just being realistic. Maybe it's time we brothers and sisters from the ghetto accept that the sister in the suburbs speaks the way she does because that's what she grew up around, not because she wants to be white. Not only do we have to accept these things, but we must also appreciate them; and this requires personal sacrifice for some. It requires personal sacrifice in that now your way of life may no longer be the pinnacle of greatness you once thought it was. Acceptance of Black America's differences might just mean that our little bubble has burst because you realize that not everyone wants to be where you are, that there are different versions of The American Dream.

Still, acceptance and appreciation becomes null and void without the compliment of proper allocation. How can the blue-collar Black, white-collar Black, and every other Black come together to benefit each other? It already does, only Black America is rarely the beneficiary. What about that Black kid from the ghetto with a horrible education, but a 42-inch vertical leap? A white university will give him a scholarship. In return, the university and others make hundreds of thousands and even millions selling tickets to see the kid play, and selling that kid's jersey in stores across America; which by the way, he will see no proceeds. Or how about the kid who can't read a contract, but he can rap. Who owns all the distribution, and who's really getting rich? White people are crystal clear on the concept of using differences to generate success. So why haven't we caught on? Now I'm in no way suggesting we manipulate each other, it's the principle of mutually beneficial relationships that is critical here. In terms of Black America, it's a matter of understanding that our social dynamic is not that different than that of whites. The minority of society controls the majority of the resources. Yet the minority needs the majority in order to produce and operate the facilities and entities which produce those resources. In other words, a few rich people own everything. But without all those who aren't rich, the rich wouldn't be rich. By and large, the financially elite Black Americans have not managed to benefit the financially less prosperous. As such, our huge and potentially dominant Black workforce is diffused and dispersed throughout the ranks of white America. There are not an abundance of opportunities for Blacks to work for Blacks. Consequently, there is little opportunity for Blacks to benefit their own communities. We are all aware of the ridiculously brief circulation time of the Black dollar in the Black community. The key is skill. Most financially secure Black Americans work for a large, white-owned corporation. Certainly this is no crime. However, said individuals are employed because they have a certain degree of skill. A person who's good with customers is going to be good whether he's an employee or an owner. My point is, it's the skill that has value, and that skill could be used in an environment that is beneficial to our communities. If a man has cooked food for a fast food restaurant for ten years, why does he not take that skill and cook food for his own restaurant, or at least a Black-owned restaurant in a Black community? The obvious barriers are capital and opportunity; two things that many Black Americans are certainly capable of addressing.

The bottom line is that we cannot expect that our needs will best be met by leaving our destinies in the hands of outsiders. That's the whole point of this whole book. We have all these forums, conventions, meetings and conference searching for the various solutions to Black America's various problems. Funny thing is, most of us already know the answers. It's just that the answer usually isn't pretty. The answer might cause us to get our clean hands dirty. It might cost us the "security" of our corporate jobs. Some white people may not like you as much. Some Black people may not like you as much. The answer requires change; and as much as Black Americans love demanding it, most of us are truly afraid of it. But then there are those who aren't afraid. So now I'm calling on you Somebody's got to be willing to step up. Somebody has to be willing to make sacrifices. Somebody has to be uncomfortable. Are you that somebody? I am.

978-0-595-35592-
0-595-35592-7